OUT of EMPIRE
the Vintage Year 1912

LTCOL PATRICK HEARN (Ret'd)

Copyright © 2025 by Patrick Hearn

All rights reserved, no part of this book may be reproduced or used in any manner including the right to reproduce this book or portions thereof in any form without the written permission of the copyright owner.

Publisher:
Australian Self Publishing Group, Pty. Ltd. / Inspiring Publishers
PO Box 159, Calwell, ACT 2905, Australia.
Phone: 61-(0) 2 6291-2904
http://australianselfpublishinggroup.com

 A catalogue record for this book is available from the National Library of Australia

National Library of Australia Prepublication Data Service

Author: Patrick Hearn

Title: **OUT OF EMPIRE:** *The Vintage Year 1912*

Non-Fiction - Memoir

ISBN: 978-1-923449-12-1 (Print)

Table of Contents

Introduction 5

PART 1: PERSPECTIVES – The Vintage Year 7
   Chapter One: The Vintage Year 15
   Chapter Two: An Edwardian Gentleman 23
   Chapter Three: 'Vivat Les Etudiants' 32

PART 2: INDIA/PAKISTAN 1912-1950 49
   Chapter Four: The Politicos 56
   Chapter Five: India: The North West Frontier 64
   Chapter Six: India: Some Frontier Campaigns 74
   Chapter Seven: India: Service Conditions 85
   Chapter Eight: India: Some Frontier Encounters 97
   Chapter Nine: India: Shikar 137
   Chapter Ten: India: The Great Naturalist 147

PART 3: UGANDA/KENYA 1955-1965 157
   Chapter Eleven: Uganda: Pearl of Africa 164
   Chapter Twelve: Uganda: The Hill of the Antelope 175
   Chapter Thirteen: Kenya: The Unhappy Valley 187

Appendices   197
   Interview with Lt. Col. Patrick Hearn (Ret) 197

A Game Of Marbles In The Khyber Pass 206
LTCOL Hugh Patrick Hearn: Medals.. 211
Cynthia and Patrick Hearn: Headstone, Southampton 212

Editors.. 213

Index.. 215

Table of Figures

Figure 1: France and Grenoble 12
Figure 2: Pat (5) and brother Charles (7) 12
Figure 3: Sandhurst Captain of Athletics 1936
(front row, third from left) 13
Figure 4: Lt. Pat Hearn, Sandhurst 1937.. 13
Figure 5: Colonial India and the Northwest Frontier 52
Figure 6: Leading a Parade, 5th/13th Frontier Force, 1938.................. 52
Figure 7: Frontier Force Patrol – Northwest Frontier 1938................. 53
Figure 8: Pat and Cynthia – engaged, India 1939 53
Figure 9: Pat and Cynthia, Marriage 10 December 1940, Bareilly....... 54
Figure 10: Baptism of First Born 1943.. 54
Figure 11: Landi Kotal Fort – Last British Commander
of the Khyber Rifles 1950 55
Figure 12: 1950s East Africa; Uganda and Kenya 160
Figure 13: Barrister and Corporate Legal Adviser, London 1954....... 160
Figure 14: Arrived in Uganda - 1955..161
Figure 15: Legal Practice, Jinja Uganda 1962 161
Figure 16: Oxford, 80th Birthday 1992 162
Figure 17: The Law for Business – 1987 and 1992 163
Figure 18: The Law for Business – 1979 and 1981........................163
Figure 19: Pat's Medals, Mounted 211
Figure 20: In Peace – Chandlers Ford Cemetery, Southampton...... 212

Front cover: On Patrol – Northwest Frontier ca 1939

Introduction

Lieut Colonel Hugh Patrick Hearn (Pat, 1912-2004) was born in a railway construction shed in Hyderabad India. He was educated at Temple Grove Preparatory School (where he was in the same class as Douglas Bader, the RAF Battle of Britain pilot) and at Bradfield School. He then went to Grenoble University in France to study law and economics.

He attended Sandhurst Military Academy and was commissioned into the Indian Army in 1936 joining the 5th Battalion Frontier Force Rifles in 1937.

He was engaged in active service with the Battalion on the NW Frontier of India (now Pakistan), in Iraq, Syria and North Africa. After attending staff college (Quetta) in 1943 he spent a year as GSO2 of an Indian Division before being appointed Brigade Major of 77 Chindit Brigade until 1945.

Service with a Frontier Force Battalion in Burma and South East Asia was followed with command of the Frontier Force Battalion regimental centre at Abbottabad.

He retired from the army in 1950 as the last British commandant of the Khyber Rifles.

Patrick Hearn then studied law at Gray's Inn and was called to the bar in 1952. The family had connections in Africa and he practiced as a barrister in Kenya and Uganda. In the late 1960s he moved to Britain where he worked as a lawyer for the Treasury Solicitors on a range of significant competition law cases and then took up positions as a legal director in industry.

After retirement in 1977 he published a number of commercial law books and spent time in both UK and Australia where most of his children lived. He married Cynthia Nicholson in 1940 who was the daughter of John Nicholson OBE a District Commissioner and Administrative Resident in India.

Pat's accounts below were written in retirement over several years; the family thought they were well worth publishing.

PART 1: PERSPECTIVES – The Vintage Year

Patrick Hearn wanted this book to be called "The Vintage Year 1912" for reasons that he explains in Chapter 1. A great year for wine and for people and for his birth. His reasons demonstrate his vision, view, humour, irony, and philosophy, in presenting the world as he saw it through the 20th century.

He notes some of the key developments towards that pivotal year of 1912, and the unleashing of a century that was dominated largely by world wars (1914-18; 1939-45) and recovery, along with the global political, economic, and social resets, including end of empire, that dominated that recovery.

This book presents the thoughts and impressions of one man, a rather unusual character of remarkable resilience, intelligence, perception, and communication, in navigating the century. We "editors" have edited only to a minimal extent, convinced that his views should truly represent him and his times, while his writing is superior and clear, when compared to much modern mulch.

Some of his views and stories may lack political correctness in that mulch, but his view of the world was devoid of the woke overlays of our current world, and the reinterpretation of modern history through rear-view mirrors. We don't mess with that, or with him.

The book includes the reflections and views of Patrick Hearn through four distinct phases of his career. First, his assessment with the century overview; a picture of his "guardian" and adviser – his father had returned to India in 1919, after 5 years as a leading military engineer in the trenches; and a vivid picture of student life in Grenoble.

Second, as the century develops, two major platforms and disruptors for Patrick Hearn were his military service, prematurely ended after the war and Indian Independence in 1947; and his completion of his mid- career in East Africa from 1955-65. He never stopped, going on in England to be a government and corporate lawyer, and then a published business writer. The years 1965-2004 are not included in this book, although the book was written between 1980-2000.

It would be easy to take the view that Patrick Hearn's life was just another who rode the waves of "End of Empire". Of course, there is a strong and unavoidable element of that. But look under the surface. His time can be better understood as "Out of Empire" or "After Empire". He trained Pakistan army officers to take over after partition, and was the last British Commander of the Khyber Rifles.

He served government in Uganda in developing Foreign Direct Investment in tourism, primary industry, and textiles. He trained Indians and Ugandans to take over and always spoke with great respect of them. In return, the Indians, Pakistanis, Ugandans, and Kenyans liked and respected him.

He did not always speak so highly of the British politicians who cut and run in catastrophic flight in India (Mountbatten's 1947 withdrawal leading to up to 2 million deaths, arguably avoidable with greater statesmanship); and in Africa (Macmillan's lesser but perhaps equally perfidious "winds of change" speech in Cape Town in 1961) when a more measured and strategic management of withdrawal may have avoided some dictatorships, wars, health and economic disasters.

Patrick Hearn was a scholar, who in different circumstances might have scaled the heights of academia; a gentleman, with firm principles that on occasions led to his losing, when dealing with scoundrels; a husband, with an incredible wife Cynthia Nicholson who followed the flag, fought for and supported her young; and a father of 5 and grandfather of 12, who was proud and supportive.

NOTE. Due to the significant historical dynamics, we have provided short, additional introductions to help orientate Part 2: India/Pakistan, and Part 3: Uganda/Kenya.

Editors.

John Patrick Hearn, Sydney 2024; Gordon Bruce Hearn, Noosa 2024.

Acknowledgements

We thank Pat and Cynthia's adult children: Susan Oakley (Southampton), Simon Hearn (Canberra), Mary Hooper (Canberra), Paul Hearn (London), and John Hearn's sons Bruce Hearn (San Francisco) and Adrian Hearn (Melbourne) for assistance in access to documents and advice and proofing.

Figure 1: France and Grenoble

Figure 2: Pat (5) and brother Charles (7)

Figure 3: Sandhurst Captain of Athletics 1936 (front row, third from left)

Figure 4: Lt. Pat Hearn, Sandhurst 1937

Chapter One
The Vintage Year

The year nineteen twelve is often claimed to be 'the vintage year' among wine bibbers. This is because it has been accounted the best year, at least for ports and champagnes, in vinicultural history. People born in that year, and knowing of its excellence, tend to arrogate to themselves a similar excellence as representing the best among humans.

Not so of course, but it might well be fair to say that those so born were from then on to have to experience and survive over many years the most frequent and fundamental social, economic, and cultural changes of all time. It is not unreasonable to express doubt that any such metamorphoses will ever again occur on the world stage, short of chaos and extinction.

The eighty-year period of British social development between 1912 and 1992 was to embrace first the deprivations and disasters of the Great War with its grievous losses of the best of the nation's human material from which many would assert that the country has not even yet recovered. Then came 'the degenerate years' of the twenties, culminating in the Great Crash of 1929 with its resulting world-wide ruin and unemployment on a scale never seen before, or even since, having regard to its impact on every walk of life and level of society.

The Second World War with its massive upheavals and civilian involvement brought about social changes which had never before been dreamed of; it also brought to an end, during the decade which followed, to the British Empire - a cause of heart-searching ever since. There followed the loose sixties with what may be described as the 'teen-age revolution', marked by a collapse of discipline on the part of the young in wide areas of British society, resulting from unearned affluence and from weak-kneed abdication of their authority by parents, all of it cynically encouraged by the media and by politicians who should have known, and acted, better, and whose standards of integrity in terms of leadership and behaviour showed a sharp decline. Yet another and equally convulsive revolution is now, at the time of writing, fully under way. From the time of the death of the old Queen in 1901 British society at once began to undergo subtle though vigorous changes. The many years of settled calm, indeed gloom, broken only by news of 'victories' in the Crimea, India, Afghanistan, South Africa, and in some of 'Victoria's little wars', stirring enough but sufficiently remote to provoke only short lived patriotic interest, began to evaporate and give way to a new more liberal spirit now running abroad. This may in part have been brought about by the character and personality of the monarch: Edward VII, at last at sixty years of age in possession of the throne. By all accounts he knew what to do with it. In this he was greatly assisted by his popular Queen, Alix, who in spite of his amorous adventures, added great lustre to his public image which was that of a benign, good humoured, and generous minded country gentleman, whose principal interest was in sporting pursuits of a robust kind. Sandringham was his favourite residence.

Hardly to be classed an intellectual he was possessed with a keen insight into the affairs of state, and a clear and firm understanding of the role of the monarch. His flair for international diplomacy was proverbial, and he enjoyed great popularity on the continent. At the same time he and his Queen exhibited real care and consideration for the less well off and the poor, and there were many, in his kingdom. It is significant that during the coronation celebrations he gave a dinner to five hundred thousand of the poor of London.

Under the aegis of this liberal king the decade in which he ruled was significant for its changes in attitudes and achievements. It is difficult to assess the extent of the influence, direct or indirect, which the sovereign can wield in a democratic society, but at least some historians would claim that to that extent he did it all, and we as a nation have been fortunate indeed, in the face of so much lowering of standards, to have had continuity in this respect ever since.

As it was the Edwardian era was marked particularly by an upsurge of cultural activity and the emergence of new personalities which were to dominate the intellectual scene for many years, as indeed many still do. It is probable that at no time in history did so much artistic talent emerge all at once. Writers like Wells, Belloc, Chesterton, Galsworthy, Walpole and Conrad began to reach an ever widening public. Playwrights such as Shaw, Barrie, and Maugham were to experience huge success. Among musicians Henry Wood, Beecham, Elgar and Vaughan Williams found appreciative audiences among the newly prosperous middle classes, while Millais, Sargent and Sickert represented a new breed of painter.

And there was plenty for the less erudite. Inspired by the fresh atmosphere of relaxation and fun the music halls came into their own with entertainers like Wee Georgie Wood, George Robey, Vesta Tilley, Marie Lloyd, and Harry Tate. That great Russian operatic bass, Chaliapin, made his earlier appearances in England during the decade which was also to see the production of Scherazade by the impressario Diaghelev in 1911, with in the same year the performances of Nijinsky and Karsovina in Spectre de la Rose; and Anna Pavlova in the Dying Swan.

But there was the other side of the coin. The increasing prosperity of the upper and middle classes was by no means matched among the lower paid whose wages remained static in the face of ever rising prices. There was widespread poverty in industrial areas of a nature difficult to conceive of in these affluent times. At the same time, as if in response to the needs of the underpriveleged, the fortunes of the Liberal party began to revive, sweeping into power at the General Election of 1906 with 377 members as compared with 132 Conservatives. Even more significant in the light of history since, the recently formed Parliamentary Labour Party returned 29 candidates as strengthened by the support of 24 loyal Liberal sympathisers. Sir Henry Campbell Bannerman was confirmed as Prime Minister at the head of a strong administration including such figures as Haldane, Morley, Edward Grey, the young Winston Churchill, and last but not least Lloyd George, while the working classes were represented by that fine personality, John Burns. Asquith succeeded C-B in 1908, and there followed a period of political and social achievement under the benign eye of the monarch which had far reaching effects on the lives of the people.

That same year, 1906, saw the passage through Parliament of the Trace Disputes Act which provided the Unions and the Labour Party with a great deal of political clout which was to be used with increasing effect over the coming years, although some might think not always in the national or their own best long term interests. Throughout this period of reform a great deal of attention was given to the advancement of education; to much needed army reform; to the introduction of old age pensions -5/- a week at seventy, a pittance but a start and gratefully received; to the general relief of poverty and unemployment and the setting up of labour exchanges; to the establishment of Trade boards for the fixing of minimum wages: all eventually leading to the establishment in 1911 of a system of national insurance to protect workers against at least the worst effects of sickness and invalidity on the one hand, and unemployment on the other.

All these measures were given reality in Lloyd George's momentous People's Budget of April 1909 which brought about 'great fiscal changes for raising money to wage implacable warfare against poverty and squalidness', said the Chancellor. He raised income tax from 1 shilling to 1/2d in the pound on incomes over £3000-a year, and even imposed super tax! Heavy increases were levied on death duties and on the cost of liquor licences with heavier taxes on spirits and tobacco. 'Vindictive' land taxes were introduced creating great friction between Commons and Lords, and subsequently to be proved unsuccessful and therefore rejected. This, in the climate of the times, was socialism with a vengeance in spite of Asquith's claim to the contrary and that it was a mere manifestation of the long standing liberal principles dictated by Bentham and Mill. But it was a very low platform upon which society was to have to build a far more widespread distribution of wealth of which there was a great deal in the country, some said nearly seventy per cent of it in the hands of only one per cent of the population.

All these profound changes go to illustrate that there was, in the decade leading up to the vintage year, an alteration in outlook at all levels of British society. The workers were being reminded that their contribution to the wealth of the community deserved greater recognition, both in cash and in status; the middle-classes were being made to realise that Jack was at least on his way to becoming as good as his master, albeit only after a long and painful transition; and the well heeled were slowly to surrender their priveleges to an ever more paternalistic state. All this on an initially small but significant scale given impetus by the rise of a new breed of professional politician to take the place of the hitherto complacent Victorian patricians.

But while it was all going on, in 1910 the King died. The nation suffered an irreparable loss as of a personal friend. Asquith wrote: 'At a most anxious moment in the fortunes of the State, we had lost without warning or preparation the sovereign whose ripe experience, trained sagacity, equitable judgement, and unvarying consideration counted for so much'. Lord Esher, his friend and adviser, described him as 'not only a peace maker, but a peace lover'; and a known fierce radical announced, after an interview with the royal presence, 'that is the greatest man that ever I had speech of', a view he never altered in spite of many such meetings.

Through his many travels abroad, Edward came to be regarded as 'the uncle of Europe'. Here his qualities were greatly admired, even by the French who had little love for 'perfide Albion'. Eight foreign monarchs attended his funeral, including the German Emperor. His dislike of strife was proverbial and he endeavoured as far as was possible to smooth over international relations which by that time were at a low ebb, largely owing to the ambitious machinations of the Germans, although no one could foresee even then the catastrophe which was to fall on the world in a few years.

But such strife was by no means confined to the international scene. Hidden beneath the upper-class veneer of galaxies, gaiety, and gourmandise, although not directly because of it, there was social conflict and confrontation in Britain which mounted steadily throughout the decade. Lloyd George's budget proved highly unpopular among the upper-classes, particularly with the introduction of what turned out to be ill-conceived land taxes. It was thrown out by the House of Lords and a constitutional crisis of major importance developed right on the King's door. In the meanwhile Women's Suffrage, which, since 1903 had been the cause of a great deal of violence, mainly on the part of upper class ladies, led to policemen being assaulted, windows being smashed and shops burnt down, and even the sight of women chained to park railings. Wrote Hilaire Belloc:

> Once in a forgotten age;
> We kept a monkey in a cage.
> Now we have no need for pets;
> Mother's joined the Suffragettes.

The growth of the Labour Party and the new upsurge in the power of the unions inevitably led to increased industrial action. A strike of the Transport Workers in 1911 was followed by a coal strike in 1912 when the number of days thus lost exceed by far anything that had occurred before, or was to occur until all records were broken by the General Strike of 1926. In the meanwhile the strength of the Liberal government brought about increasing pressure for Home Rule in Ireland matched by a determination on the part of Protestant Ulster to stay aloof, and this gave rise to mounting difficulties which, as we all know, still persist.

But throughout all these upheavals the well entrenched upper classes still continued to live their ordered lives, many of them having little knowledge of how the bulk of their compatriots lived theirs. But that did not mean that the gentility were lacking in consideration and compassion for those less fortunate than themselves; indeed such qualities were among the acknowledged tests of gentlemen, as the character portrayed in the next chapter bears witness. With all these developments and disasters it could well be claimed that the year 1912, the vintage year, stood on the watershed of time between the settled and secure years which had gone before, and the social turmoil and economic disruption which was soon to follow.

Chapter Two
An Edwardian Gentleman[1]

Charles Arthur Sebastian-Smith, Major, Royal Engineers, retired, was, in 1912, an Edwardian gentleman of means. Like many of his well-to-do kind he had served his country wherever it had been pleased to send him until he had reached his majority in rank whereupon, this event following shortly on the death of his mother, to whom he was devoted, he reluctantly resigned his commission in order to care for his properties and possessions. These included a substantial and handsome five floor terraced house in an exclusive gardens in Earls Court; a modest but tidy estate in Shropshire; and a comfortable portfolio of stocks and shares.

With ample income to satisfy his cultural, sporting, but, by the standard set by his class of society at that time, by no means

---

[1] The Edwardian Gentleman, Charles Arthur Sebastian-Smith, was a generous and kind gentleman who kept an eye on Patrick Hearn when he was young and without much family and parental support. Patrick had returned from University in France and the depression of the 1930s was making employment difficult to find. Sebastian-Smith, a friend of Pat's father, acted as an informal guardian and advisor and was the influence that caused Pat to join the Army to make ends meet. So began Pat's Army career. Written by Pat, this chapter's vivid portrayal of an Edwardian life—lived to the fullest—sets the scene for the remainder of the book.

extravagant tastes, he entered fully into the social round. The several months over Christmas of each year he would spend shooting and hunting from his estate, moving to London in the spring. There he would base himself for the summer season, while carrying out excursions into the countryside to visit friends or to attend sporting social occasions. Always immaculately turned out and full of good cheer he would be seen at the Derby and at Ascot; at Wimbledon and at Lords; at Henley and at Cowes. The sports themselves held no very great attraction for him, but the people did, and everywhere he would spread and attract an aura of good humour and fun.

The late summer, just before the shooting season, would find him refurbishing his liver in the company of one or two cronies at Vichy or Baden Baden or some such watering place in preparation for the hospitality to be received or dispensed in the coming months. He never married, joking that if he had he would have broken too many hearts. He liked to tell the story of how, at a country weekend party, he proposed to all three daughters of the house on the same evening – and they all accepted. He had to get up early and leave by the bedroom window in order to catch the four o'clock milk train for London.

One of the Major's great delights was, when in London, and on a fine spring day, to be sent out shopping. It was an all day event. Having breakfasted off devilled kidneys and buttered eggs lovingly prepared for him by his Spanish housekeeper, and having been meticulously groomed and attended to by his 'man' who, having served as his batman in the army had no hesitation in accepting the offer to prolong the rewarding experience as his valet in civilian life, we join him as he steps out into the world on a gentle May morning in 1912. This is a special occasion being a few days before and preparatory to his forty fifth birthday when he is to give a sumptuous dinner party to which he has invited those eleven persons, all male, who have shown him the greatest kindness during the years.

Leaving the door of his house we see him as a cherubic, exquisitely turned out figure, his healthy rubicond face decorated with a well trimmed, delicately pomaded, cavalry style moustache. To relieve the sobriety of faultlessly cut dark grey worsted suit he sports a light canary coloured waistcoat with spats to match, thus setting off his heavy black brogues, highly polished: including the soles. His shiny black bowler hat, his cravat in his old school colours, and his silver headed malacca cane bearing his regimental crest, complete the impressive picture of the man about town.

Stopping at the corner of Warwick Road to buy a button hole from his old friend the flower lady, the while exchanging pleasantries with the local copper who hails him a hansom cab, he rides in state the length of Cromwell Road until deposited outside his club at the corner of Piccadilly and Down Street. Entering the bar to partake of a sherry and bitters, lay a few bets with the porter, and swap badinage with a few of his chums, he emerges once more on the street and 'au pas militaire' sets out for Fortnum & Masons, first pausing by the new Ritz Hotel to enjoy the fine vista down St James's Street to the Palace and its clock by which he sets his gold half hunter.

Inside this august establishment, founded in 1814 and very much the centre of London high society, our major orders, among other delicacies, a Strasbourg Pie, some Bath Oliver and Rich Traveller biscuits, and a Stilton cheese. A story about this emporium concerns a young man of exquisite taste for everything except danger. Early in the 1914 war, not being in uniform, he was approached by a lady, handed a white feather, and asked whether he was prepared to fight and die for his King and country. He replied: 'No. I have no wish whatsoever to die for my King and country, but I am willing to shed the last drop of my blood for Fortnum and Masons'.

At Jacksons of Piccadilly, almost next door, he buys some fresh marinated tunny fish, a madiera cake, and various exotic fruits. Then on he goes down the street, passing Hatchard's famous bookshop, there since 1801; and St James's Church, designed by Christopher Wren and built in the latter half of the seventeenth century. Opposite is the Royal Academy, founded in 1768; also Albany, once the home of Lord Melbourne, and later that of the 'Grand Old Duke of York', he of the thousand men, until converted, in 1802, into bachelor's chambers where a man could live in style, as did Byron, Gladstone, and Macaulay, who there wrote part of his 'History of England'.

Crossing the top of Lower Regent's Street, and leaving the Criterion Restaurant on his right, Sebastian makes his way to Scott's at the north west corner of Leicester Square. It is time for his mid-morning snack. This consists of a plate of whitebait and a glass of stout. Suitably refreshed he retraces his steps to the top of the Haymarket where, not far down on the left, he enters the bow windowed shop of Messrs Fribourg & Treyer, purveyors of tobacco, cigarettes and snuff. Here he orders a box of Corona cigars, some Egyptian and Turkish cigarettes, and a few packets of his favourite snuff.

On down the hill to His Majesty's Theatre where he books two stalls for a new show, then, cutting across St James's Square with its stately buildings, our major sets a steady pace along Pall Mall, leaving on his left what had been Nell Gwynne's house at no 79, conveniently situated for visits by Charles II whose favourite place of residence was St James's Palace some two hundred yards distant. Turning up St James's Street Sebastian passed on his right three old established and exclusive shops: Messrs Lobb, the bootmakers; Lock, the famous hatter; and Berry Brothers & Rudd, wine merchants, who date back to the seventeenth century. Proceeding on up the hill past Brooks Club on his left and Boodles on his right, he reaches his immediate destination. Mounting the steps of White's where he is to take luncheon with friends, we lose sight of him until around four p.m. when, well topped up with vintage port, he emerges to be carried happily home in a hansom cab.

Little did he or his contemporaries realise at that time that in little over two years something would happen at a place called Sarajevo, which they had probably never heard of, which would fundamentally alter their way of life and the gracious and easy going environment which they enjoyed. After four years in France which left him a martyr to asthma, he returned to find that the maintenance of his estate in Shropshire was no longer possible in the face of increasing taxation, low agricultural returns, and the high cost of maintaining tenanted cottages. With a heavy heart he sold out, and at the same time had his town house converted into flats, keeping for himself the ground and first floors and the basement which he had elegantly done up and furnished as a cosy sitting/dining room and a bedroom. He was thus able to live in tolerable comfort, while retaining the services of his faithful housekeeper and valet. No great hardship, one might say, but the change epitomised the adjustment in social values which from then on was to accelerate, as we shall later discuss.

But in the meanwhile we are still in the vintage year when Sebastian, Bassy as he was known to his closer friends, was much in demand at shooting house parties given by the landed gentry. This was partly because of his skill at bringing down the birds: he liked them fast and high, the latter for both shooting and eating, and partly for his entertainment value. He was possessed of a fine baritone voice and a skilled and delicate touch on the piano upon which he would allow himself to be persuaded to perform after dinner much to everyone's enjoyment. He had recourse to a wide repertoire ranging from serious works by composers such as Chopin, Mendelsohn, and Grieg, to lighter music from the operettas: Florodora, The Gipsy Princess, The Geisha, and The Chocolate Soldier, popular songs from which he would sing to his own accompaniment.

But what Sebastian really enjoyed most was his rendering of ballads from the music halls, mainly suited to all male audiences being as risqué or as vulgarly amusing as Edwardian custom at the time permitted. It is an indication of the impression made by these performances that after sixty years there is no difficulty in remembering some of them word for word. One concerned the ever popular day at the seaside and went like this:

> There's something in the seaside air,
> that makes you feel that you don't care.
> There must be something in the seaside air,
> that makes you want to do the things you do do there.
> What is it makes the girls so bright and breezy,
> wanting to be cuddled everywhere;
> what makes the things with trousers on

follow the things with blouses on:
there's something in the seaside air.

Another was more sombre:

I went down to the Rose and Crown,
stayed there till I got tight;
the potman came and turned me out,
I turned to go, my nearest way
was through the old churchyard.
None of my friends would come with me,
I thought that rather hard.
While wandering midst the old grave stones
I heard somebody call;
I turned and lo! a dozen ghosts
were sitting on the wall.

By the end of the first post-war decade Sebastian was entering into old age by the measures of that time. But, although both financially and physically subject to increasing limitations, he retained his generous and light hearted outlook on life, continuing to entertain, and to be entertained by, his many friends, while losing none of his wit and ebullience. At about this time someone presented him with a black half Persian kitten. Already of well developed proportions the friendly little animal grew to become what the Major, who doted on him, described as 'the heavyweight champion of the gardens'.

One night our major was having his supper when there was a knock on the front door. It was a policeman who was carrying the cat in his arms. 'Excuse me, Sir' he said 'but I know this is your cat. He has been been behaving very strangely, going round the gardens into one area after another and making a lot of noise. So thought I had better bring him home'. Sebastian laughed: 'That's alright, constable, we sent him to the vet this morning, so I expect he has been going round cancelling all his engagements'.

Then fate struck a dreadful blow. Buster (that is what he was called) disappeared. Word went out, a reward was offered, and everyone in the vicinity kept a look out, but to no avail. There was no trace of the cat, whether alive or dead. The old gentleman grieved over the loss of his companion. Then, about a year later, something happened. Walking along the gardens one morning Sebastian noticed a black cat which by its general appearance closely resembled the missing Buster. He called it by name and it hurried across to him. Taking the animal home the Major decided on an identity test. At the top of the house there was an attic room where the cat liked to sit, waiting for the unwary mouse. Leaving it there he descended to the basement, prepared some food, and then called Buster. To his delight down it came, went straight to the place where, traditionally, its bowl was placed, and ate up its meal. It was Buster alright.

The cat was in an emaciated state and clearly distressed. The vet came and, after examining the animal's paws, said that it had walked a long way, probably a hundred miles or more, living off the land as best it could, determined to make its way home as it had. Plenty of love, affection and good food soon restored Buster to health, although from then on he never left the precincts of the house. In any case he, like his master, was getting old, and it was a fine sight to see the two of them: the Major sitting by the fire in his studded leather wing chair, eyes closed and puffing at his huge carved meerschaum pipe; the cat sitting on his lap and reaching up across the old man's chest, its arms round his neck and the back of its head resting against his cheek, a picture of bliss and contentment.

The old gentleman died quietly in his sleep at an advanced age. His funeral was attended by a throng of people of all ages and from all walks of life. Utterly truthful, generous and compassionate, he was never heard to say an unkind word about anyone. Noone knowing him could have grudged him the happy and, by the standards of the time, modestly prosperous life it had been his acknowledged good fortune to live. But behind all his good humour and wit he concealed, during the last fifteen years of his life, a deep sadness. He grieved for the friends he had left behind, many of them lost in the mud of Flanders; even feeling a sense of guilt that he had been spared. And he grieved also for the hundreds of thousands of young men, the flower of Britain's heritage, whose lives had been sacrificed, thus leaving a leadership gap at all levels of society the effect of which on the future of the nation has never been truly assessed, nor perhaps could it be.

Chapter Three
'Vivat Les Etudiants'

The effect of the sudden transition of an idle youth from the easy-going, somewhat boring, environment provided by an English public school in the late nineteen twenties to the heady climate of a French university has unfortunately to be described by that vulgar word: traumatic, as the necessity arose to apply an Anglo-Saxon nose to the Gallic grindstone. The instrument selected by fate to bring about this painful metamorphosis was Maurice, Professor of Literature at Grenoble University, a man of immense erudition, humour, charm and, from time to time, severity. His ability as a teacher could hardly have been bettered. Charged with the formidable task of steering me through the dreaded international baccalaureat, he applied himself with a mixture of didactic skill, encouragement and 'the boot', to achieve ultimate success.

After some eleven years of being crudely 'taught' at prep and public schools, that short year stands out as the only time in my life in which I was well and truly 'educated' to the use of intellect and the enjoyment of culture, and with them a taste for learning which has never left me. It was a memorable experience, the more so as I was privileged to live at the professor's home and under his guardianship, as one of his family. This consisted of his wife, a redheaded beauty of obvious Viking ancestry, hailing as she did from the North; and two children: Michel and Monique, adding another while I was with them. Thus I was enabled not only to achieve proficiency in the language in a surprisingly short period of time, but also to become thoroughly absorbed into the French way of life and thought, and weaned away from that tiresome insularity which used to be, and to some extent still is, a clogging feature of the British character.

Not infrequently Maurice and I would walk together the mile or so to the Lycee where I would take my place in the class reserved for foreigners to be taught the usual crop of general subjects which in those days made up the secondary curriculum. In the class we had a fine assortment of international talent. There were students in ones or twos from Spain, Italy, Sweden, Siam, Persia, Bulgaria, and even one from Equador who wore plus-fours, among others. In the course of our brisk walks Maurice would regale me with anecdotes larded with philosophical comment. Sometimes these were aimed barbedly at some alleged blemish in the English character or customs of which he was no admirer.

He told with obvious relish the story of how he had been invited to give a series of lectures at Oxford University. Crossing the channel he arrived at Dover where he repaired to a restaurant. 'They brought me some of your Roasted Beef and Yorkershire Pouting. Degoutant! Epouvantable! I got back on the boat and at once returned to France. Nevaire again will I visit votre pays sauvage'. On Sunday mornings he would don black overcoat and a black hat to go to church. On the way back his sensitive acquiline nose would twitch as he passed each house so that he was able to announce to his wife that M. Dupont at numero 11 was to have for his luncheon a 'pot au feu'; M. Blache would be eating roast pork with prune stuffing; and Madame Martin had a 'casserole of duck'. These claims were almost certainly fictitious and served to remind his wife of what he would like to see on his own table soon. As it was, Sunday luncheon was a rare feast whether for the food; or for the wine, which was carefully chosen to suit the repast, well chambré and much discussed; or for the conversation which was invariably lively and stimulating, sometimes hilarious.

Given good weather Sunday afternoon was no time for slumber. Instead the family auto was rolled out, Madame and the baby sat in front; the other children, including me, were bundled into the back, and off we went at high speed, which never seemed to vary with circumstance, into the hills. The Professor prided himself on his skill at the wheel. With enormous pleasure he would negotiate bends in the road by the execution of 'des traverses magnifiques' about which he would boast for days after, the meanwhile prompting Madame to protest: 'Mais Maurice! les enfants!' I could not have agreed with her more.

The importance of their language and literature to the Gallic peoples was such as to surround any professor charged, as was Maurice, with its impartation with an aura of dignity and glamour which he accepted with a natural modesty. At the same time he carried out his duties as a lecturer at the university with obvious enjoyment, and it was sheer entertainment to be witness to his discourse on the relative merits of Corneille and Racine in their treatment of certain passages of common application. The propositions he put forward got the full treatment of flowery rhetoric as he literally gloated over the rich sequences.

But life under his tutellage had its drawbacks. After finishing at the University or Lycee in the late afternoon I was required to return to the house without delay and there to work non-stop until half past seven - no time for 'le fifoclock'. Furthermore I had to exhibit all my written work, and there was plenty of that, for the stern and uncompromising comment of my master, whether or not the subject matter lay within the bounds of his particular responsibility. But out of all this austerity I found a friend. Her name was Marie Louise and she was an elderly Savoyarde peasant. She was also the household cook and probably unbeatable at her craft. Almost toothless except for one long, sharp, and brown stained eyetooth which jutted out over her lower lip, she presented a somewhat grotesque image, concealing, as is so often the case a heart of gold and a sharp native intelligence.

Aromas from this lady's concoctions would creep tantalisingly up the stairs inviting my descent to the kitchen where I was allowed to remain provided that I cut things up and ran various errands, and kept out of the way while she presided over the preparation of whatever culinary perfection she had planned for the evening's menu. In so doing I made the detailed acquaintance of many succulent dishes, some of which have remained firmly enshrined in my kitchen repertoire ever since. One of these is a 'coq au vin', a dish too often reduced by Philistines to a tasteless gooey chicken 'bugger-up' of little gastronomic merit.

To do it properly: For four discerning persons take two fair sized fresh chickens. Joint and skin them. Over a hot stove fry them in about one third of a pound of butter in an ample saucepan with some chopped garlic, plenty of finely chopped parsley, seasoning and a generous dash of brandy. Cook for about twenty minutes adding a sprinkling of oregano and some mace or nutmeg. Then add a large chopped onion and about half a pound of sliced button mushrooms. Cook for a further ten minutes. Then add a half pint of tarry red wine - a Spaniard might do, into which has been blended a generous tablespoon of cornflour. Reduce heat and simmer for a further five minutes until cooked to perfection and ready for transfer to a casserole. It is important then to lay across the top strips of lightly cooked smoked bacon, then leave covered in the oven at a medium heat until ready to enjoy. Crisp potatoes please, and preferably some sauteed baby carrots, and you have a 'Coq au vin a la mode de Marie Louise de Savoie'. And the wine? A robust Beaujolais, or better still a Chateauneuf du Pape with its subtle bouquet of violets.

It was part of the system at French universities that their lecturers, in addition to carrying out the duties relating to their particular specialist subjects, often took classes in other subjects at Lycees. Thus it came about that, being the sole member of our cosmopolitan study group to be offering classics, I found myself learning Latin in a class of French youths, the teacher being none other than Maurice. He bided his time. Came the day when we had, by way of 'prep', been given to study a piece from 'Tite Live' (Titus Livy). When the moment arrived for someone to translate he uttered the dreaded words: 'Notre jeune ami brittanique va traduire' and I was on my feet feeling lonely and conspicuous. The Latin presented no great problem but from the moment I opened my mouth I had the assembled company rolling in the aisles with my execrable English accent which was, if anything, even worse than Winston Churchill's.

But as if under fire I kept going while Maurice looked on and listened impassively making no attempt to control the uproar. When I eventually sat down he uttered only one word: 'bon' and the episode was closed. But I thought I detected a certain malicious gleam in his eye. At the same time the experience acted as a stimulus towards a mastery of the language which was, of course, his intention.

Love of their language tended to cause French men of standing to indulge in exaggerated eulogies which would be frowned on by the more prosaic Britons. It came about one fine day that I found myself summoned, along with a number of others, to attend on Monsieur le Proviseur - the headmaster - in the Assembly Hall. We had been selected to receive 'les felicitations du Proviseur' for meritorious work and behaviour. This marked a change for me as never before in my scholastic career had anybody ever said anything nice about me or my work, rather the contrary. We all stood there while the head treated us to a discourse extolling our many virtues and urging us to even greater achievements in the future. In case, however, we might take this too much to heart and head he was diligent in stressing that it was not only to us that the credit for such brilliance must go. Oh no! Most must go to our parents whose undoubted talents and parental example will have contributed largely to our success, and would no doubt continue to do so in the future. This went down a treat with those parents who had come for the occasion and who were distributed around the back of the Hall.

Mention of this habit of linguistic opportunism brings to mind an incident which took place in a remote part of the Syrio-Turkish frontier during the War. The Taurus Express, which plied between Baghdad and Istanbul, was standing at the frontier customs post.

On board were many German nationals being repatriated from Persia which had recently fallen into Allied hands. Perhaps needless to say each one was being subjected to rigorous search by the Free French customs officer. He had just about finished when a German woman screamed out that her purse containing a lot of money had been stolen. Something of a panic ensued until the immaculately clad officer, who had been busy questioning the person suddenly and uninhibitedly plunged his hand down between her voluminous breasts, where he had detected a neck cord, and withdrew it clutching a bulky purse. It was of course the missing money. Enraged at the insult he drew himself up to his full, not inconsiderable, height. 'Madame' he said with acid contempt 'When you get back to Germany you may tell your friend, Monsieur Hitlaire, that you have had the honneur de parler with an officer of the Free French Army'. With that he saluted with a flourish, turned smartly about, and marched off, leaving the lady in tears and the rest of us rolling, not in the aisles, but in the corridor.

One of the problems facing a renegade public schoolboy, accustomed as he was to strenuous daily exercise, was the absence of organised games. This was something which had no place in the French calendar. Nevertheless upon enquiry I was told that there was indeed a game of rugby to be had on a Thursday afternoon. Clad in blue shorts with vest and stockings in my old school colours I duly presented myself at the stadium to which I had been directed. I found a few far from elegant persons dressed in their normal day clothes, their trousers secured at the ankles with bicycle clips, some with cigarettes dangling from their mouths, aimlessly booting around a mis-shapen rugger ball. That was it.

Further enquiry revealed that there was a private rugby club which went by the name of 'Les Rats'. I applied to join and in due course was invited to turn out for a game. The players were clad, as to their nether parts, in very short thin, almost threadbare, and very dirty blue cotton pants. On the right buttock, in a suggestive position, there was sewn a large rat in grey cloth. One character, in the back row of the scrum, had in addition a prominent red heart attached to the left side. The significance of this was obscure, but I feared the worst. The smell emanating from the ruck was overpowering and could not be described with any accuracy without giving deep offence. At one point I was put in possession of the ball, but was quickly tripped up and then jumped upon with both feet by a gentleman who, from his girth and general appearance, can only have been a professional all-in wrestler. The final whistle, almost the only one to be heard in the game, came not a minute too soon and brought to an end my short lived French rugby career.

After the match both teams met in a nearby cafe. This involved imbibing copious quantities of hot red wine and lemon, and singing repeatedly songs like Valentine, Aupres de ma Blonde, and something which went:

Nous qui sommes des AS
Nous avons des ananas - nanas- nanas
Nous avons des ananas
(**In English**:
We who are AS
We have bananas, bananas
We have bananas)

(Apparently the Gallic reply to our 'Bananas - yes we have no). As one man they adjourned to the brothel while singing lustily, or more like lustfully:

Vivat les etudiants, oui
Vivat les etudiants,
Its ont des femmes mais pas d'enfants
Vivat les etudiants.
On s'en fou .....(the rest is unprintable)
(In English:
Long live the students, yes
Long live the students,
They have wives but no children
Long live the students.
We don't care...)

There was once an American student who paid a visit to one of these establishments were he appears to have loved well but not altogether wisely. Three days later he discovered that he had need of medical treatment. He was directed to an address where he was told he would find a pox-doctor, but when he got there he found that it was a shop situated in a street, with a lot of other shops. There was nothing to indicate any particular function except that in the shop window there was only one article. It was an elegant and obviously very expensive lady's watch displayed on a pedestal in the middle. Entering the premises he found that it was indeed what he was looking for, and after being attended to he enquired of the doctor as to why he exhibited a lady's watch in his window. The doctor looked at him wryly and, with a typically Gallic shrug of his shoulders, replied: 'Monsieur, que voulez vous que je mette dans la vitrine?'

Entry to the University proper brought with it a fair measure of freedom, at least outside study hours. By the time the average French youth has passed his 'bacho' he has acquired, in contrast to his English equivalent, the habit of work, so that if one was to achieve anything and avoid rustication it was necessary to keep up the pressure throughout the year. Attendance at all lectures without fail was essential. But there were plenty of wild parties and other activities to relieve the monotony, principally among the foreign students, the French tending to take themselves more seriously. But some of the activities witnessed were essentially French in character.

There were three or four cinemas in the town. These had traditionally conceded a fifty percent discount to students. Owing to excessive rowdyism and general bad behaviour this was stopped. The students' union called on the management to restore the privilege – or else, but without success. Action therefore had to be taken. The largest and most central of these establishments was the Royal. Word went out that on a certain evening at a given time as many students as could manage it should congregate in the square outside the place, and when the time arrived a large crowd had gathered. A car drew up and from it was removed and taken into the cinema a huge sack. This was opened and to loud shouts and catcalls there emerged a veritable cloud of bats which invaded the auditorium and effectively emptied it. Called upon to change its mind the management refused. The next night it was pigeons which revealed that when excited they have little control over their nether functions. Once more the management obdurately refused to surrender - 'do your worst' they said. The students did. A few nights later an even larger crowd had gathered, many with dogs which they had been asked to bring. What with fights and other doggy activities all hell had already broken loose when a car drew up carrying an even larger sack than before. Rats. A whistle was blown, the sack was opened, the dogs were released, and pandemonium ensued as the terrified rodents sought sanctuary inside the cinema with the dogs in hot pursuit. That was enough. Management capitulated and student power prevailed. But it was hardly cricket!

Students' parties tended to occur spontaneously and were not always very gentlemanly affairs. The mixture of nationalities ensured the emergence of many different tastes and indisciplines. At one classic about thirty students of both sexes had assembled for an impromptu binge in a large first floor apartment belonging to a Scandinavian nobleman. In no time it was well out of hand. The pianist, a huge Prussian who sang loudly from a large and vigorous Teutonic repertoire, interrupted his performance from time to time by slamming down the keyboard cover, standing up, and shouting at the top of his voice: 'What time does der fonckink begin?' This was illustrated by the crudest possible gesture made with his massive forearm and fist. In one corner of the room an American professor on a visit, later in life to become internationally known as an evangelist, had organised a game of poker with a stunningly good looking group of his female compatriots, the stakes being, one by one, the ladies' garments. One wondered what would be the jackpot. In another corner someone was ladling out some powerful concoction from a large blue-flowered chamber pot. Near the door a small British contingent, probably destined for the Foreign Office, conspicuous and self conscious in dinner jackets, stood po-faced and vaguely disapproving.

Suddenly a door opened and there strode into the room the Nordic host. He was stark bollock naked. He had fallen asleep in his bath and not realising that there was a party had come in search of a drink. Suddenly becoming aware of the presence of ladies, and true to his gentlemanly instincts, he took a short run and dived headfirst out of the french window, not, assumedly, being aware for the moment that he was not on the ground floor. At that the party temporarily disintegrated as everybody except the pianist, who continued to perform, rushed out and down the stairs to the foyer only to be met by the awesome sight of the recently airborne gentleman coming through the revolving street doors, totally unconcerned, and still in the 'altogether'.

Parties given by French residents were, of course, a lot more sedate, and only the most 'suitable' foreign students were invited. Among the young ladies of the haute bourgeoisie the 'surprise party' was at that time all the rage. This required that a group of males would foregather at some rendezvous, each of them armed with a bottle. At a given time the party would advance upon the apartment where the anticipated hoolie was to take place, and someone would ring the bell. A fair ringletted beauty would open the door: 'Aaah... quelle jolie surprise, alors!' and everyone entered like a Macedonian phalanx. Spirits drooped however when they reached the drawing room which had been cleared, and the floor liberally chalked for dancing. For there, in serried ranks, around the wall, exuding a strong smell of lavender - it might well have been formaldehyde - sat the 'meres de famille', there to keep a stern eye on their daughters and to see to it that there was no hanky panky. These ladies were presided over by Madame la Generale, a fearsome mustachioed figure with pink hair and wielding gold lorgnettes which she rested on her ducal proboscis. There was to be no dancing cheek to cheek nor anything else at all adventurous.

The cosmopolitan character of the university brought together a wide variety of types, male and female, with greatly differing social and cultural backgrounds and political persuasions. In the early thirties, at the time we are talking about, the Russian revolution had occurred little more than a decade ago, while the Great War had left behind a legacy of social upheaval so that monarchies and aristocracies all over Europe were beginning to tremble, particularly in the face of events in Germany. Everywhere people were on the run and underlying everything there was a sense of pending catastrophe brought about by a general unease which the Great Crash of 1929 had done nothing to relieve. Inevitably any seat of learning must house people with strong subversive leanings and sinister intentions, and no continental such establishment was immune. The presence under one roof at that time of representative of forty seven different nationalities created conditions in which hidden pockets of propaganda and intrigue developed.

Meetings took place in the guise of social gatherings in students' flats and hostels. These to a well brought up young Englishman were as boring as they were distasteful and largely incomprehensible. Nevertheless studying at such a place led to the need to consort with all types and kinds as part of the educational process, if nothing else. At one such party, attended at the invitation of a Hungarian doctor of economics some twenty guests arrived furtively as if plotting an assassination. A Rumanian woman with spots and pervasive body odour first lectured us on the evils of capitalism and the iniquities of the Jews. She was followed by a tall lanky French student, a poet and a notorious pederast, with a rich plummy voice activated by a highly mobile Adam's apple, who inflicted on us a long drawn out recitation of a home-made piece of verse entitled 'On Frappe a la Porte'. On each occasion when he did 'frappe' it there was opened up a new line in sedition. The evening's entertainment was concluded by a Polish renegade priest who roundly condemned all religion or any rules of conduct other than those imposed by the State, as we sat on the floor sipping fiery slivovitch and trying to eat some particularly revolting garlic sausage, at the same time as endeavouring to stay awake and appear interested.

It will have been an awareness of all these unhealthy continental goings on which inspired potential employers in Britain to shun graduates of foreign institutions as maverick characters - there were not many of them - vaguely tainted with left wing sentiments and therefore unemployable. After a long and searching job-seeking interview at an office in Regent Street I was told by way of brush off by the chairman of a prestigious company that if I was proposing to seek any further such interviews: 'Take my advice and don't tell anyone you were at a French university; and for heavens sake don't say that you read economics'. That brought to an early end all hope of a city career for which I had seemingly been trained, or for that matter any career at all. There were reputedly three million unemployed in the country and prospects were bleak. There were men among the working class who had been out of work for as many as eight years and were no longer employable. The dole for a single man was fifteen shillings, for a married man twenty one with a few shillings added for each child.

Every class of society was affected by the depression which had been steadily deepening since the war ended. The 1929 crash had impoverished many middle class families thus depriving many school and university leavers of that measure of support then deemed necessary to launch a young man on a business or professional career. London and other cities were full of trained men only too ready to accept one pound a week to get a start, but that they could only do with family backing, at least to the extent of providing a home. Those lacking this luxury were in dire difficulties. The safety net normally provided by the dominions and colonies in the past was no longer available. North America and Australia were closed to all immigration, having even worse problems of their own, and to go to South Africa one had to have fifteen hundred pounds. What a hope!

Against this background I had to consider myself fortunate, in the Autumn of 1932, to have found a menial post with an American company in the City. My take-home pay was twenty seven and sixpence a week. For that I had to work as little more than an office boy from eight thirty in the morning - and not a minute late - to six o'clock in the evening, and until twelve noon on Saturdays. The rent of a bare attic room near Regents Park was ten shillings a week without gas for lighting and heating which was metered at a shilling a time. To save fares mostly I walked to and from work although the cost of shoe repairs posed a problem. My breakfast and luncheon consisted of a cheese or ham roll and a cup of coffee in a 'café'. But I was saved from moral and material ruin by the fact that, immediately upon return to the U.K. I had joined a London Territorial regiment. Most nights I attended the drill hall where, in addition to finding warmth and companionship, I was well exercised. What was even more important I could obtain, for the sum of one shilling and sixpence, a generous plateful of meat and veg, and even some pud to follow, and a pint of wallop cost only fourpence. Thus I was able to keep body and soul together but there was little left over for clothes and other requirements and the situation could not last.

PART 2: INDIA/PAKISTAN 1912-1950

As was often the case in those times, Patrick Hearn and his older brother Charles were born in India to (later Colonel Sir) Gordon Hearn, a brilliant officer of the Royal Engineers, himself from a family with long links to India; and Lady Olive Carew Hyde Cates, likewise with India links. The marriage was not a success, and the world war and other turmoil at the time can be held partly responsible.

Charles went to Australia initially doing farming work and in later years serving as a technical specialist in defence weapons research, while Patrick was captain of sports and graduated from Sandhurst to join the 5/13 Frontier Force Regiment of the British Indian Army. It is notable that Patrick met and married Cynthia Nicholson in India in 1940. She was a daughter of John Patrick Nicholson of the Indian Civil Service (ICS – the heaven born), who was a grand nephew of Brigadier General John Nicholson "the Hero of Delhi" who led the charge that broke the siege of Delhi in 1857, ending the mutiny – and was killed in that assault.

This background is mentioned to exhibit that the family on both sides was deeply committed to India and expected to remain serving as India developed in its road to nationhood and independence. In the meantime, there were cataclysmic changes in play as the war ended with the atomic bombs. There was the non-violent movement led by Ghandi; the political jousting of Nehru and Jinnah - including Nehru's personal links with both Lord and Lady Mountbatten; and the desperate attempts of the postwar Attlee Labour Government, first for a United India and then for a separate India and Pakistan.

Perhaps inevitably, Lord Mountbatten's brief stewardship and premature withdrawal led to at least two million deaths as Hindus and Muslims migrated to spurious safety, many being slaughtered in trains and while marching. Ironic indeed that later in 1979 in Mullaghmore, the IRA blew Mountbatten sky high.

In this maelstrom, Patrick Hearn and his colleagues fought to preserve the integrity and discipline of the integrated Indian army, and then to train the leadership of the new, separated armies of India and Pakistan. As Commander of the Regimental Centre in Abbottabad (very near to where Osama Bin Laden later met his end in 2011), and as the last British Commander of the Khyber Rifles in Landi Kotal Fort on the Afghan border, he continued to serve. Leadership is service – a rare principle today!

Patrick Hearn's Indian and Pakistan career ended in 1950 following partition and his continuing service to train the Pakistan Army officer corps while holding active command. He arrived in a still bomb-scarred post-war England in 1950, deciding to resign his commission from a soon to be cut back army, and to study for the bar exam as a barrister at Gray's Inn, achieved in 1952. He concluded that he could not break through as a barrister with the flood of younger lawyers coming through, so he worked successfully as a legal counsel with companies in engineering and brewing.

In 1955, Patrick and Cynthia decided that they would not be able to educate their four children to the standards they wanted in England. Patrick looked wider, as fitted his explorative, entrepreneurial way, and accepted a senior legal and business development post with the Government of Uganda.

"Pull out, pull out on the long trail – the trail that is always new." (Rudyard Kipling)

Figure 5: Colonial India and the Northwest Frontier

Figure 6: Leading a Parade, 5th/13th Frontier Force, 1938

Figure 7: Frontier Force Patrol – Northwest Frontier 1938

Figure 8: Pat and Cynthia – engaged, India 1939

Figure 9: Pat and Cynthia, Marriage 10 December 1940, Bareilly

Figure 10: Baptism of First Born 1943

Sitting: (L. to R.):- SUB-MAJOR BALOCH, LIEUT. COL. H.P. HEARN, BRIGADIER D.H.J. WILLIAMS, O.B.E. H.E. SIR AMBROSE DUNDAS, BRIGADIER HISAM-UD-DIN, MAJOR J.M. PENLY, MAJOR QAYUM

Figure 11: Landi Kotal Fort –
Last British Commander of the Khyber Rifles 1950

Chapter Four
The Politicos

Of the many attributes with which Henry Lawrence was generally credited perhaps the most outstanding was his ability to choose the right men for the many daunting tasks which presented themselves during this period, and to earn their love and respect. These men were the "politicos": hand-picked for their courage and intellectual resilience, soldiers turned administrators who, resting on their personality and drive, were able to bring law and order and a form of government to the different and widespread areas of the new province. Their names are still known, and even cherished by the many European and Indian civilians and soldiers who followed them and profited from their example, but hardly at all in their own country where fame was neither sought nor recognised. There was Herbert Edwardes of Bannu fame, described by General Roberts as "one of the most remarkable men the Indian Army has ever produced"; Harry Lumsden who had formed and who led the famous Corps of Guides; Frederick Mackeson, to be murdered by a fanatic in Peshawar in 1853; James Abbott, Commissioner in Hazara, who had become famous for his journey to Russia via Bokhara in 1839 to bring about the release of Russian prisoners kept in slavery by the Turkomans. But it has generally been conceded that of all these striking personalities the most outstanding was John Nicholson. Born in Lisburn, Northern Ireland, in 1822 he was the son of Doctor Alexander Nicholson, scion of an old Cumbrian family, who started life as a Quaker but was later expelled from the Society for marrying outside it. Like so many of his contemporaries in India John was deeply religious although equipped with a fiery temper. Men said that he went to war with a bible in one hand and sword in the other; ruling over a wide district around Peshawar he inspired a traditionally truculent and uncompromising people with admiration and affection tinged with fear at the sound of his name, and even more at the sight of his presence. Those were the days when ruthlessness in the service of God was considered right and proper as conferring security and justice on the great majority of law abiding citizens. Lord Roberts wrote: "Nicholson impressed me more profoundly than any man I had ever met before, or have ever met since. I have never seen anyone like him. He was the beau ideal of a soldier and a gentleman." From such a man this was praise indeed. John Nicholson was mortally wounded leading the attack on the Great Burn Bastion during the storming of Delhi in 1857. The historian Trotter describes him thus: "Cast in a giant mould, with massive chest and powerful limbs, an expression ardent and with a dash of roughness; features of stern beauty, deep set hazel eyes, long brown beard and a sonorous voice. There was an air of immense strength, talent and resolution in his whole bearing, a power of ruling men on high occasions of which none could fail to be aware." In the course of British Indian history there may not have been many like him, but there were plenty of runners—up as we shall see.

The presence of British troops in the province, and the expense of maintaining them which fell on the Sikhs; the increasing influence in the country of the British administrators with their imperious and strong willed attitudes towards certain social customs; and the inability of the Sikhs to forget their bruised pride, led inevitably to another conflict. But in the meanwhile the resignation of the gallant and wise Sir Henry (now Lord) Hardinge was greeted with dismay coming as it did a mere three years after his appointment as Governor General in 1844. As was stated at the time "the distribution of his patronage was regulated by an exclusive regard to the interests of the public, and he was as free from the suspicion of nepotism as his predecessor (Lord Ellenborough). In India, by his plain, good, common sense, by his decision of character and kindly disposition, together with vigour of discipline, he secured the golden opinion of all men." His successor, James Andrew, Earl of Dalhousie K.T. Lord Clerk Registrar of Scotland became Governor General in February 1848 and there commenced an era of immense economic development which was to lead to the eventual unification of the country. But first the Sikhs had to be reckoned with, and that urgently. The first sign of the trouble to come occurred at Multan, that city of heat, dust, beggars, and graves, where the Hindu Governor, Mulraj, having developed ideas of independence, refused to hand over the revenue to the puppet Sikh government. Two British officers who were sent to remonstrate and collect were foully murdered, and a punitive force was despatched; but before this the heroic Herbert Edwardes, then a Lieutenant and later to be Governor of the Punjab, had laid seige to Multan with a small and heterogeneous army: "bold villains who were ready to risk their own throats, and cut those of anyone else." Desultory though heavy fighting took place between May and September 1848 when reinforcements from Lahore and Ferozepur, including a detachment of crack Sikh troops led by their best General Shere Singh, arrived to form a strong investing army under a distinguished gunner officer, General Whish. Called on to surrender Moolraj made reply with a cannon shot at the General which very nearly hit its target.

The citadel at Multan was of immense strength, and all the makings of a lasting confrontation appeared to be present. The situation was not improved by the defection to the enemy of Shere Singh and his men which added considerably to the anxiety of General Gough, still Commander in Chief of the Company's army, who almost daily expected a new Sikh attack in strength in the Ferozpur area; a view which was reinforced by the departure from Multan of Shere Singh himself in October. It was not until mid-January 1849 that Multan finally fell by which time the Second Sikh War was well under way. Towards the end of November 1848 Gough had marched northwards from Lahore with the intention of crossing the Chenab River where Shere Singh had taken up a defensive position on both banks at Ramnagar with a force of thirty five thousand men. Here Gough decided on attack and, with his usual "up Guards and at 'em" technique launched his cavalry across open ground and deep sandy soil which, after being driven back across the river by the first charge, the Sikhs met with shattering musketry fire, while well sited Khalsa artillery on the flanks played havoc with the British guns. On the 1st December a British encircling attack from higher up the river arrived at the enemy position to find that Shere Singh anticipating the move had withdrawn from

Ramnagur, and a counter attack was threatened. After a sharp exchange Shere Singh, with his troops in good fettle, fell back on the River Jhelum where he had organized an exceptionally strong position and where he no doubt expected to fight and win his decisive battle. By now he could muster forty thousand men and sixty two guns.

No amount of embellishment by Gough could give an impression that the battle at Ramnagur was other than a defeat for British arms, but worse was to follow. After waiting six weeks for Multan to fall and thus make available fresh reinforcements, Gough marched on the Jhelum where, allowing his native impetuosity to over ride the need for careful reconnaissance, he once more ordered a frontal attack. Then all hell broke loose. The battle of Chillianwala (the Sikhs called it Rassul) was fought on the 13th January 1849; it cost the British twenty six officers and seven hundred and thirty one other ranks killed, and sixty six officers and one thousand four hundred and forty six other ranks wounded. The use of cavalry in thick country ahead of the artillery, which thus had no field of fire, exposed them to heavy punishment from the enemy guns, and in the midst of the general confusion a strong body of Sikh horse took the main body of British cavalry in the centre putting them to flight so that the guns were overrun and four of them captured before nightfall put an end to what must be accounted a defeat, in spite of greater Sikh casualties - or so it was reported - and in spite of contrary opinions expressed by Lord Gough, who was compelled to withdraw his army some two miles, among other reasons to obtain water for his suffering troops who were half dead from exhaustion. Four British guns were captured; the colours of three regiments were lost; the reputation of the British tarnished; and the Sikhs proportionately elated. Marshman wrote: "By the community in India it was considered a great and lamentable calamity. The intelligence of the combat was received in Britain with a feeling of indignation and alarm. British standards had been lost; British cannon had been captured; British cavalry had fled before the enemy, and a British regiment (the 2nd Warwickshires) had been annihilated. These disasters were traced, and justly, to the wretched tactics of Lord Gough, and he was recalled with the full approval of the Duke of Wellington."

Luckily for Gough, before he could be replaced by that forthright character Charles Napier, conqueror of Sind in 1843 and victor of the famous battle of Meeanee fought with great ferocity against the Beluchis: "Thick as standing corn, and gorgeous as a field of flowers...", he was able to claim a fine victory over the Khalsa army at Gujerat, assisted by the arrival of the erstwhile beseigers of Multan, and by some timely advice from Henry Lawrence that the adroit use of artillery in this form of warfare was preferable to the onslaught of naked infantry, however disciplined and brave. Shere Singh, forever resourceful and unexpected, moved his force, now estimated at sixty thousand men including some fifteen hundred Afghan horse, and fifty nine pieces of cannon, to the rear of Gough's army of twenty five thousand troops and one hundred guns. Gough moved against them on the 21st February 1849 and found them in a well chosen position with well protected flanks, but with the artillery carelessly exposed. Having learnt his lesson Gough opened the proceedings with a mighty cannonade inflicting great destruction and carnage among the enemy guns which had revealed their positions by opening fire at too long a range. Meanwhile Shere Singh's favourite weapon, the cavalry, had been deployed on either flank and after some stern fighting had been out-manoeuvred. At this Gough ordered forward the redoubtable British infantry which, in spite of severe casualties, carried the defences at the point of the bayonet repelling continual cavalry attacks, and eventually surrounding the main body of the Khalsa infantry in the village pouring in musket fire and causing the most dreadful slaughter. The Sikhs, after exhibiting their usual bravery and tenacity, could do nothing but flee, hotly pursued by the victorious British cavalry. The battle was won and Chillianwala avenged. Shere Singh, having shown great brilliance in command marred only by the fatal mistake of failing properly to conceal his guns; and who knows by what other agency this may have occurred; retreated behind the Jhelum River with only a relatively small fragment of his once splendid army. The Afghan contingent fled north closely pursued by a British flying column under Sir William Gilbert, who chivvied them up to the awesome gates of the Khyber Pass, where reluctantly but prudently he drew rein while the quarry wasted no time in returning to their base. Local comment had it that "those who rode down the hills like lions, now ran back into them like dogs."

On the 12th March 1849 Shere Singh surrendered his sword to General Gough. His soldiers walked forward one by one and, after kissing their weapons threw them on the growing pile, many of them in tears, before setting out for their homes resigned to a feeling of proud submission to a power that proved stronger than themselves, and one which they would loyally and bravely serve for nearly one hundred years to come. The Punjab was annexed to the British Crown; so was the Koh-i-Nur diamond, the Mountain of Light, taken in 1823 from Shah Sujah by Ranjeet

Singh, which John Lawrence absent mindedly put in his waist coat pocket and subsequently forgot. When asked to produce it there was a panic stricken search which ended when his servant handed over what he thought was a piece of glass which he had fortunately put away. Men of Lawrence's moral outlook thought little of such baubles. With the end of the Second Sikh War the whole of the Indian sub-continent became subject to the rule, direct and indirect, of the Company acting as agent for the British Crown. The construction of roads, railways and canals according to a national plan was now feasible and in Dalhousie the country had the right man to lend imagination and vigour to these enterprises at the same time as creating an administrative service with men drawn from both civil service and the military and described as "the flower of the service, men of mature experience, or of noble aspirations for distinction." It was under their influence and by their example that eight years later soldiers of the Punjab, when the Mutiny broke out, not only remained true to their salt but fought at Delhi, Lucknow and Cawnpore, and elsewhere to avert what might have been a great calamity. In all these happenings the Khalsa were prominent. One can only marvel at the nobility of character of such men, so recently defeated and deprived of their independence, who far from taking advantage of a dangerous threat to their new masters in order to extract vengeance for past reverses, strove so valiantly to secure and advance their interests.

Chapter Five
India: The North West Frontier

The newly hatched subaltern, standing on the steps of Sandhurst in the early thirties, and looking out for fields to conquer, would have seen very little to attract him. Everywhere, it seemed, the 'pox brittannica' (Churchill) reigned. Service in the British Army in England had little to offer, particularly to an officer without private means as was often the case. Reasonably to live and to enjoy a measure of social and sporting activity in those days required a private income of the order of three hundred pounds a year, while in the posher outfits such as the Guards or Greenjackets a lot more was needed. Mess bills alone could come to more than an average officer's pay.

This sort of money is of little significance in these affluent times, but in the inter-war years it stood in the way of service careers for those whose fathers and grandfathers had spent lifetimes in the army or navy with little to pass on except honour and perhaps a little glory. In those days, not so very long ago, money was not a prime factor in the choice of a life's work.

From the end of the Napoleonic War until the outbreak of the Great War service in India offered fine opportunities of achievement and distinction to the English gentry. The decade following on the cessation of hostilities in 1918 saw a decline in the popularity of the Indian Army among many of the families which, now by long tradition, sent its sons to serve there. This in no way resulted from the performance of the Indian soldier which, tested and tried so often before, reached its peak in France, at Gallipoli, and in Palestine. It seemed to derive from a war inspired disillusionment with army life on the one hand, and on the other, a good deal more importantly, from a realisation that political changes might be imminent so that any new entry might not enjoy a lasting career. And so it turned out.

However, by the thirties India, in spite of all the doubts, again became popular among Sandhurst cadets, and there was no shortage of applicants from among the more promising. Many of these were attracted principally by the fact that in all the world the only place which seemed to offer any chance of active service was the North West Frontier which, over a hundred years or so, had earned for itself a glamourous place in military history, and where fame if not fortune was still to be achieved, also an early grave. The alternative was life in some dreary garrison town in Britain, engaged in routine administrative duties when not standing on a chilly fog-ridden parade ground, listlessly watching those few men in the company available for parade after allowing for guards, duties, and fatigues. Indeed, at that time, the whole of Britain seemed to be in the grip of boredom and deprivation with high unemployment and little apparent prospect of improvement.

As has been indicated, officers in the British Army received scant pay and allowances. What was worse promotion, being organised on a regimental basis, only came when vacancies occurred. There were instructors at Sandhurst in the thirties who, after some thirteen or fourteen years service, were still Lieutenants. By contrast, in the Indian army not only was pay a good deal better, but subject to passing the necessary examinations, promotion to captain came automatically after eight years service, and to major after sixteen. But it has to be stated that not all officers took kindly to the sort of study necessary for success in the exams. One such, attempting to make his way up the ladder, but finding himself busy in other ways, chose the night before sitting to enquire of another officer what books he recommended him to read.

Another attraction offered by Indian service was the variety of occupations available to officers who might feel in need of change, or a widening of experience, thus enhancing their prospects. There might also be a little matter of additional monetary allowances to satisfy the needy. Examples were Frontier Scouts, service with tribal militias, popular but selective; the Burma Rifles; Indian State Forces, such as the Bikanir Camel Corps, reserved perhaps for those cavalry officers with a better seat on a camel than on a horse. There were also jobs going as Adjutant to European manned Territorial Forces such as the famous Calcutta Light horse, and so on.

So our eager young subaltern, having chosen a career in the Indian Army, and having been fortunate enough to secure a place in a Frontier Regiment might, within a few days of arrival, have found himself lying behind scant cover on the side of a hill being shot at by a gentleman with a wheaten complexion, a prominent hooked nose, eyes like a hawk, and a modern Lee Enfield rifle which he knew how to use with determination and precision so as to remove from the world at least one Feringhi. Perhaps the latter might wonder if he may not have made too hasty a decision.

To the majority of the good citizens of England the north West Frontier was a remote environment in which impoverished young men played at being soldiers. In fact it was a thorn in the flesh of British imperialism from the time, in 1849, after the second Sikh War, when the whole of the Punjab from Lahore up to the jaws of the Khyber Pass, the gates of hell, came under British rule, until 1947 when the British Indian Army finally withdrew from tribal territory, not without unfriendly exchanges with the no doubt exhilarated tribesmen in hot pursuit.

It all started in 1839 when, by courtesy of the Sikhs, who then ruled the Punjab with a rod of iron, the so-named 'Army of the Indus', having made a long detour through Baluchistan, invaded Afghanistan. The purpose was to remove from the throne the Amir, one Dost Mohammed, who had been flirting outrageously with the Russian Bear, always a threatening shadow, real or fictitious, over India's northern borders, and to replace him with a puppet king. The invasion of the country turned out to be a relative picnic. But it was a case of 'come into my parlour'.

True to the British tradition of making oneself at home in other peoples' countries, the Army settled down to an easygoing cantonment existence. Ladies arrived from England to join their husbands and to organise the social round. But it did not last. Revolts occurred in different parts of the country until, in November 1841, the storm broke in Kabul. There then took place the famous retreat of the greater part of the army towards India under the most appalling conditions of cold, hunger and thirst as can be imagined, being chivvied all the way by Afghan tribesmen. Only one officer, in the last stages of exhaustion, survived to ride in to the British outpost at Jalalabad bringing the shattering news of the disaster.

An 'Avenging Army' was quickly formed under General Pollock with the additional duty of recovering the many hostages, including women and children, who had been left behind. It reached Kabul in September 1842 after inflicting severe casualties on the Afghan forces. The hostages were recovered, the Kabul bazaar blown up, and, profiting from previous experience, the Army promptly turned round and marched back to India while still in one piece, the 'powers that be' announcing, prematurely as it turned out, that never again would they become involved in the internal affairs of Afghanistan. The Dost, in captivity, expressed astonishment 'that the rulers of an empire so vast and flourishing should have gone across the Indus to deprive me of my poor and barren country'.

In spite of this partial recovery of prestige, the whole episode had severely dented for the time being the aura of invincibility with which so many past victories had surrounded the British forces. This may have contributed to the waging of war by the truculent Sikhs a few years later which was to witness some of the bloodiest battles ever fought by the British on Indian soil. The subsequent annexation of the Punjab in 1849 presented the British Indian government with a problem which was never to be fully solved for the next one hundred years. This was how to control the independent Pathan tribes who inhabited the mountainous strip of country, about fifty miles wide, which ran from north to south forming a natural barrier between India, trans-Indus, and Persia, Afghanistan, and any other more northern menace to the country's peace and security. These Pathans, although related to the Afghans and speaking more or less the same language, were totally independent of all outside interference. For hundreds of years they had exercised tight control over the approaches to Hindustan which lay principally through the Khyber Pass and by way of the Kurram valley further south. Tribute was exacted from all travellers, either in cash or kind, for the right of passage and for 'protection'. Hidden away in the wild hills of the Tirah, and other tribal strong holds were fortified villages organised for defence more against each other than against intruders from outside who could only penetrate in considerable force, if at all as we shall see. Either through feuding or battle life for a Pathan tribesman was never far removed from death.

The tribal territory of the Worth nest Frontier can be divided into a number of reasonably well defined areas, each inhabited by tribes or sub-tribes of the same ethnic origin but of differing characteristics. All were capable of fighting with great ferocity, fearlessness, and skill; all were capable of dreadful acts of cruelty, often inflicting appalling tortures on their captives in war. At the same time they had a certain rigid code of honour, a ready sense of humour albeit sometimes misplaced, and a gay nonchalance which commended itself to many British soldier-administrators thus creating a guarded friendliness between the races. However trust was not a word to be used in describing this. History militated against it. There is a Mahsud proverb: 'Tell no man where you are going, the time you are starting at, or the amount of money you are taking with you'.

Furthest north of the tribal areas in terms of military involvement was Chitral, not as it happens inhabited by Pathans but by Mongol/Chinese tribes. Some one hundred miles to the south lay the Malakand Pass giving entry to the regions of Buner, Dir, Swat and Bajaur, all Pathan strongholds housing, among others, the warlike Yusufzais, with whom Alexander the Great had to contend with no little difficulty as he led his fighting columns into India in 326 BC. Further south still, immediately to the north of Peshawar, was Mohmand territory, scene of some fierce fighting over the years, notably in the nineteen thirties when Field Marshals Auchinlech and Alexander, each then commanding infantry brigades, had their first experience of fairly large scale battle command.

Immediately to the west and a mere ten miles from Peshawar stood the infamous Khyber Pass, twenty seven miles long and dominated by the Tirah to the south. Some of fiercest battles ever fought by the British on the Frontier took place here. The principal occupants of the Pass, and of the precipitous Tiran hills were the Afridis, regarded by many as the natural aristocrats among Pathans. Indeed they possessed a certain relative sophistication which might be attributed to their more frequent contacts with the outside world than history had afforded to other tribes. An important instance of this was the presence of the Greeks over several centuries, both before and after the birth of Christ, in the plain of Peshawar and in the colonies north of the Hindu Khush, while the constant, stream of travellers over the course of centuries will have contributed further to their enlightenment. Nevertheless they were, and no doubt still are, fanatical adherents to the Muslim faith.

Proceeding southwards we come to the garden city of Kohat on the other side of the Tirah, guarding the route to the Kurram valley which ran alongside Afridi and Orakzai territory. Here in the valleys live more settled tribes such as the Khattaks, the Bangash and the Turis, all excellent material for service in the army and in frontier militias. Another one hundred miles to the south is the garrison town of Bannu, the take-off point for

Waziristan where live the Wazirs, and the dreaded Mahsuds whose capacity for cruelty, treachery, and truculence had probably no equal on the Frontier, or for that matter anywhere else. The last stop on our southern pilgrimage, during which we traversed some five hundred miles and visited the abodes of some ten principal tribes, is Dehra Ismail Khan which used to be a place to be avoided if possible.

All the five military bases we have mentioned: Malakhand, Peshawar, Konat, Bannu and DIK are situated along the line of the Indus, and is settled, that is to say, in non-tribal territory. This did not stop marauders from entering them by stealth for purposes of murder or thievery, often both. These bases housed support troops and regional headquarters: infantry brigades, horsed cavalry, artillery, and ancillary units, supply and transport and the like. There were also RAF squadrons, notably at Kohat and at Peshawar. Since the adoption, in 1922, of what was known as the 'Modified Forward Policy' as distinct from the Forward one which had in the past led to unsuccessful attempts to establish a military presence in Afghanistan, a number of strong points had been established also in the middle of tribal territory, the object being, in short, to try (the operative word) to strangle at birth any major rising of the tribes at the same time as sending out from time to time as necessary punitive columns to destroy crops and villages in cases of local misbehaviour. There was plenty of that.

Thus in that same year the fortified camps at Razmak and at Wana were constructed and strongly manned, and a British Indian Brigade posted at Landi Kotal at the head of the Khyber Pass and thus on the Afridi's doorstep and only three miles from the Afghan frontier. A prize story about Razmak needs to be told.

This concerned a senior ranking German officer who visited India not long before the war in the role of Hitler's envoy. Obviously, with what his boss had in mind, he had orders to ferret out as much military information as he could get. He asked to be taken to see Razmak. This meant flying: in the rear seat of an Audax, not the most stable of craft, over some very rough territory and through a great deal of turbulence, with no small chance of being shot up the backside on the way. By all accounts he did not enjoy the flight.

On arrival at Razak the officer enquired as to how many troops were stationed there. He was told about ten thousand. 'And how many vimmin?' he asked. 'None' came the answer. There was a gasp of astonishment. 'Vot, ten thousand men and not one voman! Now I know how it is that you British have built such a huge Empire'.

This modified forward policy was finally adopted as the result of many decades of experience since 1849. Campaign followed upon campaign while those Frontier units not directly involved would be busy 'keeping the peace' elsewhere. It was not the larger scale recorded events which provided the attraction to the adventurous, but the smaller operations which gave scope for that enterprise and initiative so suited to the temperament of the young Briton of those times. There was plenty to choose from.

The first major military event to take place after the annexation of the Punjab did not do so on the Frontier but some six hundred miles to the south in and around Delhi where the main action of the 1857 Mutiny was fought out. As far as the north west was concerned the most dangerous aspect of this was the very real possibility of Afghan invasion of the Frontier Province and with it a general rising of the Pathan tribes in sympathy. That this did not happen was due to a number of factors: First the very high standard of British officer appointed to administer the area and to officer the Punjab Frontier Force. Second, the swift action which was taken to disarm disaffected down country regiments manned principally by sepoys recruited in Bengal and Oudh. Third, the raising of tribal levies to assist in controlling the region during the absence of the regular garrisons; and the departure southwards to play an important part in the fighting of a strong highly mobile force under the command of John Nicholson, whose character and personality were greatly admired by the Pathans.

Of particular significance was the fact that Dost Mohammed, long now restored to the throne of Afghanistan, held back in spite of his long standing claims to the city of Peshawar as part of his domains. Perhaps the traditional hatred of the fanatical Muslim for the Hindu whose mutiny it really was may have had something to do with it. Even the British were to be preferred! Finally a great deal of credit needs to be given to the Sikhs who only eight years before had had to accept defeat, but whose loyalty and gallantry throughout were unwavering as was to remain the case for the rest of the life of the British Raj.

Chapter Six
India: Some Frontier Campaigns

In 1863 there came the Ambela campaign, from which many important and indeed painful lessons were learnt. This took place in Swat and was sparked off by the presence there of a force known as the 'Hindustani Fanatics', mainly fugitive Muslim sepoys who had fled from the post-Mutiny retribution to form a colony in Buner where they were granted sanctuary. It started as a relatively small punitive expedition, the local Yusufzai tribe, the Bunerwals, having agreed to preserve neutrality. The force, numbering about five thousand, having arrived at the Ambela Pass after a difficult march, posted picquets two of which became famous in Frontier fighting history. These were 'Eagle's Nest' and 'Crag'. The possession of either one of these by the tribesmen would have made the whole position untenable.

Probably because of the unforeseen difficulties encountered by the column on the approach march which had reduced the fighting capabilities of an already small force operating on its own, a feat quickly recognised by the tribesmen, the Bunerwals exhibited a sudden change of attitude. Assembling in large numbers on the heights outside the ring of the picquets, they launched a series of desperate attacks on the two key posts. The tactics adopted were to become familiar to all frontier soldiers throughout the years ahead: the silent movement into position after dark until concentrated in a large number. Then, under cover of their matchlock marksmen they launch themselves with shouts and yells on the picquet to be met by heavy fire from the defenders and temporarily dispersed. Then a second even more determined attack attempting to breach the stones forming the picquet walls. These attacks to be repeated several times until, if received with steadiness and resolve as they would be by experienced frontier troops, the attacks would die out and the tribesmen withdraw leaving many dead.

This Ambela campaign provided something of a watershed in frontier tactical development. First it taught the need to guard against the total unpredictability of the Pathan; second, the importance of the construction of adequate lines of communication in order to permit swift reinforcement of men and supplies; and third, to reduce to a practical minimum the administrative tail in terms of excess baggage and non-combatants.

The year 1878 saw the commencement of the Second Afghan War which, although it entailed heavy fighting in the Khyber and at Peiwar Kotal in the Kurram, can not be classed as a Frontier campaign and therefore earns no place in this narrative. In any case it has been written about many times in different forms. Throughout the period from 1849 up to 1890 it is estimated that no less than thirty small scale expeditions took place in various parts of the Frontier, each one posing its own particular problems and teaching its own lessons. The variety of terrain and of the nature of the inhabitants was such that no set-piece encounter could ever be relied on. This tended to sharpen the wits. Indeed in 1890 the whole method of fighting became altered and very much more hazardous by the introduction into the hands of the tribesmen of the breach loading rifle. They were thus able to adopt British methods of warfare which, in brief, meant obtaining control of the heights and from there directing well aimed rifle fire at any advancing, or retiring, force. One determined tribesman, well concealed, could and indeed has been known to hold up the advance of an entire brigade.

As an illustration of the type of 'small war' in which any Frontier soldier might find himself involved at any time, albeit an extreme one, the story of the Hunza-Nagar expedition of 1891 needs briefly to be told. This took place in a remote 'shangri la' situated high up in the Himalayas in an area of snow and ice, torrential streams, deep gorges, and precipitous cliffs. A small force of not much more than a battalion was despatched under Lieut Colonel Durand with orders to hoist the Union Jack over the country, the inhabitants of which had shown truculence. The nature of the operation and the resistance encountered were such as to require the maximum of individual initiative, endurance and bravery.

Advancing from Gilgit a garrison was established at a fortress named Chalt, forming a base from which other forts and eventually the towns of Hunza and Nagar could be seized. While at Chalt Durand received a letter from the Thum - yes, that is what they called the ruler - of Hunza asking why the British had come to his country 'like camels without nose rings' and, going on: 'We will cut off your head, Colonel Durand, and then report you to the Indian Government' adding: the fortress of Chalt is more precious to us than the strings of our wives' pyjamas'. The

Colonel was not impressed and, although severely wounded in the process, went on to occupy the country.

A feature of this operation was the way in which seemingly insuperable natural obstacles were overcome by one masterly piece of engineering improvisation after another. The credit for this went to Captain Fenton Aylmer of the Royal Engineers who, true to the traditions of that Corps, subsequently led the assault on the key strongly held cliff top fortress of Nilt, earning, together with Lieut Boisragon of the 5th Gurkhas, the Victoria Cross for what was described as one of the most gallant deeds ever performed on or beyond the Frontier.

Without doubt the most important year in the whole long history of Frontier fighting was 1897 when the entire region went up in flames. The reason was largely pan-Islamic sentiment aroused by certain Mullahs, muslim priests with considerable authority over unsophisticated fanatical people. This general rising of the tribes had its origin two years before when the British fort in Chitral was invested at the instigation of a Pathan war-lord named Umra Khan. A Chitral Relief Force was hastily formed under the command of Sir Robert Low numbering about fifteen thousand troops with orders to proceed via the Malakand Pass. Once more the Swati tribesmen moved to prevent it with a force of some twelve thousand tribesmen who dispersed after five hours of heavy fighting. From then on the story was one of steady advance interspersed with desultory actions and of fine engineering achievement in which once more Aylmer, later to command the Kut Relief Force in the Great War, played a prominent part.

Another name which appears frequently in the R.E. annals of these times was that of Hunter-Weston, later to command a division in France when he became known affectionately as 'Hunter Bunter'. Probably as the result of long service on the Frontier where officer and man relationships were much closer than was usually the case, the General liked to show friendliness and concern for his troops. This did not always turn out as intended. It seems that on one freezingly cold winter's night he was standing on the platform of a railway station in Northern France seeing off a leave train which was packed with soldiers of his division. Opening the window of a carriage he called out: 'Your divisional commander wishes you all a merry Christmas'. Voice from inside: 'Then tell the silly old bugger to shut the bloody window'.

When the relief column reached Chitral it was to find that a small force under Colonel J.G. Kelly, which had set out from Gilgit the previous month, had already lifted the siege. This remarkable feat was carried out in conditions similar to those encountered a few years before in Hunza. Marching in freezing temperatures, without tents and with only fifteen pounds of baggage per man, the column crossed the Shandur Pass at over twelve thousand feet, many of the soldiers suffering from snowblindness and frostbite, and pressed on defeating the Chitralis in a number of engagements in which great ingenuity and heroism were displayed. Any one seeking inspiration from these events should read the fine epic stories of the Hunza and Chitral expeditions as examples of what the Frontier soldier might expect in the course of his service.

Two years after this, in 1897, a series of more or less simultaneous risings took place the length and breadth of the Frontier, straining for a time the resources of the Indian Army to the limit. The trouble was sparked off by a relatively minor incident in the Tochi Valley to the West of Bannu. It then spread northwards to the Malakand where desperate fighting took place against the Swatis of Ambela fame. Heavy attacks were launched simultaneously on the encampment at the Malakhand Pass and on Chakdara Fort ten miles to the northeast. In spite of suffering severe losses under the steady fire of the garrisons, the tribesmen continued their mass attacks for eight days calling forth the maximum of discipline, courage and fortitude on the part of the defenders consisting mainly of Sikhs and the ubiquitous Guides supported by the Bengal Lancers. With the formation and deployment of a Malakhand Field Force under the command of the suitably named General Sir Bindon Blood the fighting slowly died down and the tribesmen went home.

It was with this Force that the young Winston Churchill served as a war correspondent. Since 1890 more and more of the tribesmen had come into possession of modern breach loading rifles replacing the old muzzle loaders, although the latter were to remain in evidence until at least the beginning of the second World War. Given greater range and accuracy, and opportunities for greatly improved concealment, they no longer needed to rely so much on the costly mass assault by swordsmen, being able to conduct their battles using fire power like the British. Churchill had this to say: 'The world is presented with that grim spectacle - the strength of civilisation without its mercy. At a thousand yards the traveller falls wounded by the well aimed bullet of a breach-loading rifle. His assailant, approaching, hacks him to death. Here the weapons of the nineteenth century are in the hands of savages of the stone age'. To this the Pathan tribesman might have replied: 'Who are you to complain, with your maxim guns and your howitzers? If you do not like the way we fight then stay out of our country'.

Following almost immediately upon the attacks on the Malakhand, the Mohmands north of Peshawar attacked a police post. A Mohmand Field Force was raised and a punitive campaign organised in cooperation with Blood's columns further north. But it was only after much bitter fighting, with the tribesmen seizing avidly on opportunities offered by tactical errors, so easy to make in such unpredictable conditions by even the most experienced commanders.

By far the most important operation to take place in 1897, and probably for all time, was that carried out by the Tirah Expeditionary Force in the Afridi and Orakzai homelands to the south of the Khyber Pass. Since the Second Afghan War, by the Treaty of Gandamak signed by the Amir in 1879, the administration of the Pass was handed over to the British, the Khyber Rifles was formed as a policing force, and a number of posts constructed at strong tactical points along the route. In August 1897 these forts came under fierce attack by large bodies of Afridi tribesmen under the leadership of their mullahs. Strong resistance was put up, notably at Landi Kotal where a subedar shot dead two of his sons who were in the attacking force. But after twenty four hours the defence collapsed under the weight of numbers, the exhortations of the mullahs to desert, and a natural loyalty to their kith and kin. Even so many riflemen managed to make their way to Peshawar.

Obviously these attacks could not go unpunished, especially in view of the generally unsettled state of the territories. There therefore took place by far the largest operation ever to be mounted on the Frontier involving some thirty five thousand

British and Indian officers and men opposed by anything up to fifty thousand stubborn and well armed Afridi and Orakzai tribesmen. The role of the Field Force was to enter the Tirah by way of the Samana ridge from Kohat to the south, and to invade the uncharted and precipitous valleys of the region destroying villages and generally laying waste to the countryside until the Afridis might submit.

The first and most difficult task facing the Force was to penetrate the outer defences. This led to the storming of the Dargai heights which were strongly defended by some twelve thousand tribesmen. This took place on the 20th October when, after five hours struggle in which many casualties were incurred and many deeds of gallantry performed the ridge was carried by the Gordon Highlanders. By the 1st November camp had been set up in the heart of the Afridi homeland, the tribes having removed themselves, their families and cattle, into the surrounding countryside. By early December the whole region had been overrun and every valley visited and laid waste. This was not without cost as the Afridis kept up a steady harassment, shooting up camps and columns, and cutting off stragglers. Both the Northamptons and the Dorsets which had come from the 'sloth belt' in the south and had no recent experience of Frontier warfare, were led into traps from which they were able to extricate themselves only by displays of outstanding bravery and tenacity, but with heavy casualties.

Still with no sign of submission from the Afridis, and with the approach of the extremely harsh winter which could be expected in that country, the commander, Sir William Lockhart deemed it time to go. Easier said than done. As has happened many times before and since, the Force was in a position of having trodden on a hornets' nest, and of having to get out of it as fast as possible - that is if the hornets will let you. On the 7th December the withdrawal commenced. One Division by way of the Waran river encountering only light resistance; the other by way of the Bara route meeting with that determined follow-up which is the hall mark of tribal fighting skill, and with which all experienced Frontier soldiers are to a greater or lesser degree familiar. In this instance the dreadful weather conditions, continuous attacks the whole length of the column, and difficulties of disengagement leading to a running battle occasioned by the need to protect the large number of slow moving noncombatants, resulted in heavy losses, so that when, after five days of meeting with every kind of obstacle, the column arrived within the safety of the picquets set up by the Peshawar Brigade, it was totally exhausted - but intact.

Shortly after this the Khyber was reoccupied, and the posts restored. But it was not until the following April that the Zakha Khel, the largest and most bloody minded of the Afridi tribes, finally submitted under blockade. The Tirah was never again invaded by the British Indian Army, nor, as far as is known, has it been entered by any European.

This brief foray into Frontier military history may serve to convey to the uninformed reader the message that what many may have been led to regard as mere secondary operations of a routine character were in fact major campaigns and expeditions calling forth the best in courage, skill and leadership. Throughout the long years during which British and Indian regiments served on the NorthWest Frontier, a large part of their time was spent under arduous active service conditions. There was built up over those years a code of tactical practice based on a very wide variety of military situations, and a flexibility of approach calculated to cater for the use of new weapons on either side or for the application of new fighting techniques.

During the ten years following on the troublesome events of 1897, possibly as the result of the swift and sure action which was taken at the time, the Frontier remained relatively quiet. It was nevertheless at all times the scene of minor operations in one area or another giving a fair measure of stimulus to those immediately involved. The situation was once summed up by a senior officer advising his juniors that if they heard a motor cycle driving round the cantonment in the middle of the, night, they should waste no time in getting up, donning their equipment, and putting on their boots.

Trouble flared up in 1908 with the incorrigible Zakha Khel and the Mohmands resulting in 'Willcocks' Week-end War' a twenty day campaign carried on with great elan by a General of that name. Local militias recruited from among the tribes came into being at about the turn of the century, and these contributed greatly to the maintenance of trans-border law and order. Service in them held out good opportunities for independent command and action and therefore became popular with up and coming Indian Army officers. The Great War saw the departure from the scene of many of the tested and tried Frontier regiments, British and Indian, to be replaced by territorial and war raised units which would almost certainly have had difficulty in coping with any major conflagration. As it turned out, perhaps remarkably, as had been the case at the time of the Mutiny, and as was to be the case in the Second World War, except for a few skirmishes the tribes held back, possibly because over the years it had all become something of a family affair, with many Afridi, Mahsud and Yusufzai men serving in the armed forces.

No sooner was the Great War over, and the much depleted regular regiments returned to India, than the Indian Army had to face up to invasion of the Khyber and Kurram by an Afghan army about fifty thousand strong. In spite of manpower difficulties swift action was taken and a campaign which had started in May 1919 was over in June with the withdrawal of the Afghans. But the tribes had been stirred up and large areas of the Frontier were once more in turmoil, notably in Waziristan where the Wazirs and Mahsuds resumed their old habits. It was this which led to the 'modified forward policy', as already mentioned, and the permanent stationing of troops in Razmak, Wana and Landi Kotal. This resulted in a period of relative peace in those areas, but it was not to last.

Chapter Seven
India: Service Conditions

When our would-be hero joined his Indian regiment on the North West Frontier in the early nineteen thirties he would have found plenty to keep him militarily occupied. 1933 saw the Mohmand campaign in which, as already mentioned, two of our famous WW2 field marshals were involved as brigade commanders. 1936 brought what became known as the Ipi campaigns (after a Fakir of that name) in Waziristan which kept the garrisons at Razmak and at Wana, as well as less centralised units on the periphery of the area of hostilities, well exercised. In 1940 much hostile activity around Bannu brought about the highly mobile and successful Ahmadzai operation about which more later. One young subaltern, on joining his regiment at that time and place, came to the notice of the Force commander who was heard to say: 'There's a lucky young man; on active service before his balls have dropped'.

His first year in India would have been spent attached to a British regiment. Many of these had long historical connections with the Frontier, and although their soldiers would not have spent anything like the time on mountain warfare operations as their comrades in the Indian regiments would have done, and were therefore relatively inexperienced and more prone to disasters which came often and suddenly, nevertheless many had fine records and were very proud of their service there. Visitors to the Khyber Pass today, after driving up the steep road from Jamrud, the old Sikh fort shaped like a battleship, to the Shahgai plateau, may there see, on the right hand side, many badges of British and Indian regiments carved into the cliff face, thus commemorating their service in the Pass. Among those represented would be: the Rifle Brigade; the Argyll & Sutherland Highlanders; the South Wales Borderers; the Northamptonshire Regiment; the Dorsets and the Black Watch; and the Somersetshire Light Infantry. Requiring special mention is the emblem of the Royal Corps of Signals: the 'Running Boy'- Hermes, messenger of the Gods. From time to time this had to be replaced. This was because the Afridi tribesmen, sitting on the roofs of buses, rifles across their knees as a safeguard against ambush, and making their way up the Pass from Peshawar, had a habit, as they breasted the ridge, of exercising their lascivious sense of humour by sniping at the boy's bare bottom.

The tribesmen, in one might say their perverse way, respected and ever admired these British soldiers who came so far from their homes to invade their country, and who gave as good as they got, sometimes better. Many British war veterans entitled to wear a Frontier medal would probably, if asked, account themselves prouder of its possession than any of the other gongs among their hard earned 'fruit salads'. High up in the Khyber hills where, from the Cerberean peaks of Tartarra, at five thousand feet, massive deeply scarred spurs sweep down the ten miles or so to the Kaoul river to the north, there is a steep ravine. Down this a British officer made his hurried way late one evening shortly after the last war. He was commanding a strong patrol of the Khyber Rifles on its way to investigate an incident in Shilman country. At the foot of the nala he came across a small grove of pepper trees surrounded by a low well maintained wall. The trees were festooned with strips of white cloth transforming the place into a shrine. This is a not unusual sight on the Frontier where the ladies, wishing to earn for themselves many brave sons, would so decorate the last resting places of holy, or in other ways respected men and, dare one say, even women. They even tried it out on a statue of Queen Victoria but then, to many, she was a 'very nice man'.

The officer, as he hurried past in the gathering twilight, glanced over the wall and was startled to see the graves of two British soldiers beautifully kept in their well swept enclosure. Unable then to stop and note details he resolved again to visit the place so as to identify the names, numbers, regiments and dates and to make other enquiries. Unfortunately the 'exigencies of the service' intervened and he never did. There they remain, apparently honoured but unsung, almost to be envied in their select solitude amid so much wild beauty. When were they laid there? It could have been as early as 1842 when General Pollock's columns passed that way; or Sam Browne's division in 1878; again in 1897 when Sir William Lockhart re-occupied the Khyber at the end of the Tirah campaign. Units of General Willcock's force skillfully deployed against the Zakha Khel in 1908 may well have fought their way through those hills, the men being buried where they fell; or at the latest perhaps in 1919 when the invading Afghans occupied Landhi Kotal and Sagh and had to be evicted. All these possibilities give rise to nostalgic conjectures, but the fact is that the Afridis treated our dead with honour and respect.

On joining his Indian regiment the young officer would need first to acquaint himself with the command structure. For many years to come his home will be the rifle company, usually consisting of three platoons, all the men being drawn from the same martial class. He may expect to find four companies in the battalion (or regiment) each one of a different class, maybe Sikhs, Pathans, Logra Rajputs, and Punjabi Mussalmans. Each platoon will be commanded by a Viceroy's Commissioned Officer, holding the rank of Jemadar or Subedar. The second in command of the company will be the senior subedar. There will be a headquarters company consisting of Signals, Machine Guns, Motor Transport and Administrative personnel: all fighting men. He would find that the Indian soldier, although literally meeting the description of mercenary, was in fact no such thing. Unlike many of his British comrades-at-arms with their 'roll on my seven and five' attitude, he was a career soldier, holding himself every bit as in allegiance to the Raj as the British to their sovereign and nation.

The Indian sepoy who was enlisted into the army was usually possessed of some land, and this established his social status. He would come of a class with a very long tradition of military skills. Often his father, grandfather and other relatives will have served in his regiment so that his prowess becomes a matter of family pride, something very important indeed to the martial Indian. His pay as a sepoy was negligible by any normal standards: as memory serves probably not more than two or three pounds a month, most of which was sent to keep the home fires burning. Leave of two months only came round every two years, although special concessions were made when arranged marriages fell due and the omens were favourable. For the sepoy generally, and particularly in a Frontier regiment life was frugal and strictly disciplined. Usually rising at five in the morning he was kept, and would keep himself, busy throughout the day needing little direction or encouragement. His one meal a day was cooked and eaten in the evening, consisting usually of curried vegetable and an ample supply of chuppattis, the unconsumed portion being saved for the following morning. Non-vegetarian classes would normally get meat only twice a week. Games were popular, notably soccer and hockey, but volley ball, being suited to the narrow confines of Frontier posts, was also much enjoyed, particularly as virtually everyone could join in. Another popular and highly skilled sport was wrestling, no holds being barred. One commander of a Sikh regiment, no mean athlete, was wont, after dinner in the Mess, to send down to the lines for one or other of the wrestling team, and to strip off and take him on on the Mess lawn.

Soon our young hopeful would find himself commanding an outpost held by his company. It was then that he would get his first taste of responsibility and a knowledge of the men he was to serve with, probably for many years. He could expect soon to come under sniper fire and to engage in the odd skirmish. But apart from the essential need to learn the language, Urdu, and to learn it well, there was the need to cultivate the friendship and trust of the Viceroy's Commissioned Officers, particularly the Subedar 2 i/c on whom he would need to rely for advice on so many matters for a long time to come. That officer could be expected to educate and bring up his young company commander in the ways of the world as seen through the eyes of the regiment. This would be done firmly and tactfully by a man of great experience, wisdom and prestige to whom the regiment was his life.

But the corner stone of the regiment was that highly respected, dignified, and all seeing and hearing gentleman: the Subedar Major. Primarily he was confidential adviser to the Commanding Officer to whom he would report every evening having himself first had reports from the Subedars. Thus he was able to exercise a remote but highly effective influence and control over all matters affecting the smooth administration and discipline of the regiment. Always immaculately turned out his dignified presence would do much to enhance the esteem in which the regiment was already held. His advice and assistance was frequently sought in order to solve many diverse problems, not all of them of a strictly regimental nature. This brings us to the story of the adjutant's cow.

Not long after the Great War there was a regiment stationed at Attock, the huge sprawling sixteenth century fortress built by Akbar, the Great Mogul, to command the principal crossing place of the mighty Indus River south of Peshawar. Officers were permitted to have their families with them, and these included the adjutant's two young children. In order to provide the necessary milk a cow was kept. It spent its time contentedly chewing the cud in the ample grounds until one day something happened. It began to swell. It was not long before the animal had assumed a grotesque size and shape. It was unable to move its head, from which protruded its sad protesting eyes, or its legs, and its tail stuck out incongruously straight behind it, like a walking stick. For all the world it resembled a hugely enlarged piggy bank, and a crowd gathered, but no-one knew what to do.

The subedar-major was eventually informed, and his arrival on the scene brought about a respectful hush. His wise authoritative eyes took in the situation as he slowly circled the distressed animal. Then he spoke: 'Vinegar'. A bottle was produced at the double, and the contents poured down the beast's throat: He spoke again: 'Stand back'. They did, and waited expectantly. After a long pause the cow's tongue began to protrude until there seemed to be about a yard of it. Then it belched, loud and long. Next, after another pause, it farted, louder and even longer. At this point several sepoys found it convenient to disappear round the corner of the barrack, hands over their mouths, but the S-M stood there purposefully, his normal expression of benign severity never leaving his rugged face. The animal continued with this performance first at one end, then at the other, until it resumed its normal appearance and set itself to graze unconcernedly. Upon this the subedar major saluted the adjutant who had had the greatest difficulty in keeping a straight face, turned about, told the assembled multitude to go about their business, and that sharply, and marched off to go about his.

The time spent on outposts or on operations were considered no hardship, but a welcome stimulant. Back in cantonments there were frequent periods of tiresome routine. The old description of war: long periods of crashing boredom broken by short sharp interludes of intense fear - did not quite fit, but could be taken as broadly applicable if one substituted excitement for 'fear'. Often, and usually in the hot weather which in those parts lasted with a vengeance from early May until mid September, there might be only five or six British officers present with the regiment; the rest would be on leave, at the Staff

College, or in some extra regimental employment. This meant that a subaltern might find himself commanding two companies; acting as temporary quartermaster responsible for supplies; doing the job of Mess Secretary, thus catering for the needs of the inner-officer; supervising the regimental accounts; and organising sporting and other recreational facilities.

It is apparent that whether in outposts or in cantonment, cultural activities were negligible. An unkind critic once said that there were only three subjects of conversation to be heard in an officer's mess: sex, shop, and shikar. Sex can be dismissed because there wasn't any. True, officers would return from leave in Kashmir with stirring tales of bedroom derring-do, few of them, if any, true. It appeared that there lurked in Srinagar a number of obliging female characters. There was the Passionate Haystack: a blonde lady built on a Wagnerian scale. Then there was a more sinuous charmer: the Charpoy Cobra. There was also, it seems, a young lady by the name of Virgen. Possibly to avoid committing an offence under what then passed for the Trade Descriptions Act, she pronounced it with the 'g' hard as in giggle. Some wag on being introduced said he thought it time for a gin and ginger - the g's being similarly hard. Yet another was a thin flat chested girl, apparently a scion of a famous noble family, who went by the name of 'the bottomless Pitt'.

Among stories of passion and adventure was that concerning an officer who returned from the wars having heard of his wife's 'goings on'. No doubt having, like Marlborough, pleasured her three times before removing his boots, he charged her with infidelity. A colossal row ensued. When things had simmered down the lady suggested that to improve the atmosphere he might care to put on a gramophone record. The records were stacked on the floor in a corner of the room. As he bent over to pick one up, she coolly took from her handbag a delicate pearl handled pistol, and shot him up the bum. This brought to a painful end a never very promising relationship.

The exigences of the service demanded that an officer be entitled to two months leave in each year, that is in theory. Leave was in fact always regarded as a privelege, never a right. Service in certain areas of the Frontier where conditions were particularly exacting brought with it an entitlement to three months, but this was a privelege normally only enjoyed by more senior officers and married ones. One newly joined subaltern was delighted to receive a note from the adjutant which read:

'The CO is working out the leave roster for the year and would like to know your preferences'. This prompted a written request for three month's leave, preferably in June, July and August, the three hottest and most unpleasant months of the year when, as an additional attraction, Kashmir, the principal resort, could be expected to be infested with abandoned female talent or so it was rumoured.

In due course he was summoned. Spoke the adjutant: 'The CO has considered your leave application. He thinks that three month's leave in your first year is too much, but he is agreeable to two months. The matter is one of timing. There is a six week course in advanced weapon training starting in early June which the CO wants you to attend. For the second half of July he wants you to attend some classes in Pushto which are to be arranged in Peshawar'. 'Oh' said the subaltern hopefully, 'and then do I go on leave?' 'That' replied the adjutant coldly 'is your leave'. And so it was.

In those earlier days an officer was not normally permitted by his regiment to marry until he was at least thirty. In any case he would not receive any marriage allowance until that age, and with pay and conditions as they were it was an expensive pastime. In most Indian regiments the principle was that a young officer should devote the whole of his time and energies to his battalion for at least the first ten years and this tended to become a habit, many officers postponing entry into the connubial state until their late thirties, when promotion and pay allowed for more gracious living. The trouble was that the longer they postponed it the more difficult it became to find a suitable partner or, for that matter, any at all.

There were two 'elderly' majors in one regiment who had served together and shared everything for nearly twenty years when one of them, in England on furlough, sent word that he was to be married. This came as a shock to his long time companion who complained that he supposed he would have to stick velvet on the thunder box. But the real problem facing married couples in India was the separation of families. The intense heat for five months of the year necessitated a departure to the hills for all women and children and, apart from other considerations, this proved expensive. It was also an unwritten law that British children, particularly boys, should not remain in India after the age of seven at the latest owing to educational and physical development needs. Another factor was the adulation poured on such children by faithful servants which was extremely bad by way of preparation for their subsequent much tougher upbringing, designed to fit them to take their turn in shouldering the responsibilities of Empire.

This splitting of the family placed the mother in a serious dilemma. She often had to make the choice between staying with her husband in India and looking after the children in the UK, while stringent financial problems intervened. In those times air travel was not available except at prohibitive cost and the sea journey took three weeks. In Victorian times the problems were yet more acute. In those days men married late, their wives often being anything up to twenty years their junior in age. In one family the very young wife of a senior officer having, after five years of marriage, had three children, found herself faced with the need to take them home leaving her husband to soldier on until his next furlough became due after another five years, on the completion of the ten year stint which then had to be served. When he did arrive he was badly broken in health and died shortly after, leaving her to bring up the young family. She remained a widow for fifty five years. Such situations were not uncommon and formed part of the heavy price of Empire.

Where, as was sometimes the case, the wife elected to stay with her husband, then difficult matters of guardianship arose. These were sometimes solved by grandparents or other elderly relatives with whom school holidays would be spent, not always with much enjoyment on either side. Another result of these long separations was that parents and children tended to grow apart. In particular fathers, unconsciously perhaps, came to resent the fact that while paying the piper they could not call any tunes in respect of the education and general upbringing of their own children. This often had the result of turning them against them, sometimes with disastrous effect on the children's lives. They became the orphans of Empire.

As indicated finding a partner often presented problems. For some this was solved by the presence in many stations during the cold weather of what was unkindly known as 'the fishing fleet'. This consisted of young ladies visiting parents or relations or family friends while on the look out for a good catch. Others preferred to wait for furlough, some eight months home leave which came round every four years or so. One officer, having become engaged to a fair damsel while on such leave, had the temerity to give her name and address to a brother officer so that he might in turn find a partner from among her friends. The arrangement was cut short by the officer 'hi-jacking' the affianced one and claiming her for his own. It is interesting to record that no serious umbrage was taken, and that the men continued to serve together in complete amity for many years. Clearly the regiment came first.

Around about the turn of this century there was a Sapper officer who, approaching forty, decided that a lonely bachelor existence was no longer acceptable to him. There were no known candidates for his affections so that he announced, as he proceeded on furlough, that he intended to marry the first decent looking girl he would meet on arrival in England. On leaving the train at Victoria he found that he had run out of tobacco. He went to a kiosk and was served by an attractive young lady whom he asked out to dinner. She accepted and a few months later they were wed. In spite of the narrow social prejudices of those times, especially in British Indian society, the marriage was a marked success, and she played a considerable part in promoting his subsequent highly successful career.

Chapter Eight
India: Some Frontier Encounters

Not so very long ago there was a notable admiral. A man of great extra-service experience founded on exceptional learning and insight. Asked his opinion as to the overall cause of Britain's problems he replied: 'we are no good at big things. Our big ships in the war-time navy were handled no better, and probably worse, than other combating nations, but when it came to the small ships, our destroyers and submarines, not forgetting units of the merchant navy, all of them commanded by relatively junior officers, we excelled. The same applied to the special forces: the commandoes, the cloak and dagger units, and the long range penetration groups. This is in the Viking spirit and tradition. What England needs is a multiplicity of small enterprises managed by younger people of talent of whom there are many in this country, but for whom insufficient scope is offered'. These were wise words, and for many who have put them to test, true ones.

One place where these conditions could be said to be met was the North West Frontier of India. As we have seen in previous chapters, throughout the many years in which the British kept watch and ward over this turbulent area, opportunities for the exercise of initiative and responsibility by junior officers of independent spirit abounded: Thus to command a company in a Frontier regiment stationed more or less permanently during 'peacetime' in an active area of the NWFP was probably the most rewarding period of an Indian Army officer's service. Various famous generals have written of their preferences as to size of command, some favouring a division, others a brigade or battalion. But to find oneself trusted to lead a company of some one hundred and twenty Indian soldiers on active service, all fit in mind, wind and limb, and highly trained, disciplined, and experienced in a wide variety of testing adventures, is to sample the finest that service life could offer in terms of independence of action, responsibility, fitness and health, and absolute trust and liking between officer and other rank: in one word, fun.

Such an experience, under such conditions, fell to the lot of the author, and lasted for some six energetic and rewarding years. The men were Sikhs, built like the trunks of trees, to whom soldiering, with all its apparent deprivations, was the essence of life. The Sikhs are not in fact a race. They are a religious brotherhood bound together by common and distinctive beliefs, and a proud history. The word 'Sikh' means a disciple, a follower of the Gurus, or teachers, of whom, between the birth of the first: Guru Nanak Sahib in 1469, to the death of the last, Gobind Singh in 1708, there were ten. The established creed was that there existed one supreme God, whose worship was open to all classes of men, and whose blessings might be shared by all persons worthy of them in a spirit of equality, independence and self-reliance founded on tolerance, honour, simplicity and clean living.

Each of the Gurus added flesh to these bones until the fundamental principles of Sikhism were expounded as: 'loyalty; gratitude for favours received; philanthropy; justice; impartiality; truth; honesty; and all the moral and domestic virtues known to the citizens of any country'. All cant and humbug are excluded. These principles stand as a moral target, and to those well acquainted with these people the influence is clear. Lord Curzon, the great pro-consul, stated that 'the standards of personal and family honour and self-respect that prevail among the Sikh community are of a very rigid and uncompromising character'. Anyone privileged to command such people soon found this to be true. Their gallantry and perseverance in the face of many years of cruel oppression in protection of their religion are matters of history which should inspire those who tend to waver in the upkeep of their own inherited principles.

During the ten years or so leading up to the commencement of the second World War a great deal of fighting took place, mainly in Waziristan, against the Mahsud and Wazir tribes under the overall direction of the notorious Faqir of Ipi, and his principal Lieutenant Mehr Dil. Much of this had a religious motive allied to a permanent resentment at the presence of foreign troops on tribal soil. Sudden attacks on outposts, on isolated working parties or supply vehicles, and on regular forces engaged in the routine opening up of communications, sometimes led to the despatch of relatively strong punitive columns for the purpose of destroying villages and crops and thus bringing the tribesmen to battle. The latter was no easy task bearing in mind the mobility and hardihood of the Pathans, their tactical sense and knowledge of the country, and their consequent ability to melt away when seriously threatened.

In contrast the movement of any Army column tended to be slow and ponderous and totally predictable, largely resulting from the use of camel transport, essential to the carriage of the mass of impedimenta necessary to keep such a column in the field for any length of time. The commander of a company in any such expedition would find himself frustrated by the need to spend long hours holding a static protective position on commanding heights, aimed at preventing attacks on the main column as it proceeded in stately formation along the valley below. At the same time he would be conscious of the fact that the tribesmen would be watching for any relaxation of vigilance giving the chance for a sudden attack which, if successful, could throw the whole operation into confusion and disarray.

Of far more interest to the officer and men of any such company was the prospect of independent mobile action of one sort or another testing all the skills and fitness attained in the course of past operations and training involving a high degree of leadership, speed over the hills, intelligent use of ground, and coordinated tactical movement. In this chapter it is proposed to recount the details of a number of such operations as an indication of the opportunities now and then coming the way of the eager young officer which did much to relieve the monotony attached to formal frontier duties, and thus nourish morale.

Before embarking on such an exercise it is important that the nature of the terrain over which such activities took place should be understood by the reader. From previous chapters it will be realised that along the whole length of the north west frontier there was no area which could be accounted immune from disturbance, but of particular geographic importance to the overall conduct of watch and ward operations on the Frontier at that time was a veritable robber's den known as the 'Ahmadzai Salient'. This feature consisted, as of course it still does, of a huge, wild, broken and precipitous area thrusting out into the Bannu plain, with its settled farms and villages, and following the administrative boundary between settled and tribal territory in a wide fifty mile arc surrounded by lofty and in many places inaccessible hill features pierced here and there by deep ravines giving access and egress to the inhabitants, many of whom made good use of them in carrying out thieving raids on settled villages and then bolting for cover when pursued, and taking refuge in their mountainous hideouts.

The occupants of the Salient, and no doubt their 'guests' from other tribal areas, had been a thorn in the flesh of the administration for many years during which no major expedition aimed at curbing their activities had, for one reason or another, been mounted. As will be recounted Nemesis struck shortly after the commencement of World War II when the whole of the area was invaded by a Force consisting principally of two highly experienced Indian Army Brigades under the command of a general notorious for the vigour and insight with which he approached his tasks. The purpose was to open up the territory to control by civil armed forces by means of the construction of roads, and the tactical siting of strong defensive posts; to punish the inhabitants for past misdemeanours by limited 'scorched earth' activity; and to warn them of the results of any future shortcomings, thus releasing the regular forces for service in overseas campaigns of which there were to be several choices.

The campaign which followed turned out to be highly successful. From a central stronghold sited deep inside the Salient mobile columns were sent out to 'search and destroy' in successive areas of the territory, returning to base within a few days, thus reducing the administrative 'tail' in each case to an operable minimum. Speed of movement was the order of the day – each day. These short sharp forays gave ample scope for the exercise of initiative and leadership by the more junior officers, commissioned and non-commissioned, while providing a refreshing interlude to the hum-drum garrison or protective duties which normally occupied much of the soldier's time. The following accounts of a number of actions and events may provide a realistic picture of some of the challenges met with by our particular company.

These include: first, the recovery of a pranged aircraft and its pilot under threat from tribal territory; second, the night crossing of the Baran river; third, a night ambush which failed; fourth, the storming of the Grang heights; fifth, the defence of the Grang picquets; sixth, the tale of a sniper's bullet and a gallant charger; and seventh, the Lone Ranger, a DIY tribesman.

(a) The Pranged Aircraft

The continued misbehaviour of the Ahmadzai Wazirs in the period leading up to the launching of the invasion of their territory caused the authorities to impose a blockade over the area while carrying out bombing raids on crops and villages. The aircraft employed, being Audaxes and Wapitis, bore little resemblance to the sleek fast machines which were soon to take to the sky in Europe. The armament was limited to a machine gun and four twenty five pound bombs which did little real damage, but they served as a potent irritant while exacting a high degree of skill and courage on the part of the pilots. This activity was supplemented by the manning of border posts at various entry points on the perimeter of the Salient from which the countryside could be patrolled for the interception of armed gangs, and of camel convoys carrying supplies to the interior. This led to frequent skirmishes.

There came a day when our Sikh company was occupying a remote post at the northern end of the Salient. A message was received to the effect that an aircraft had been seen losing height over tribal territory, apparently in difficulties. Only an approximate location was given, and the orders were to search, find, and if possible bring home, particularly the pilot who would stand to lose a great deal more than his life should the tribesmen, who would certainly know that something was up - or down, get to him first.

It was five o clock in the morning when we set off down what was little more than a cart track which ran parallel to tribal territory and a mile or two from the towering escarpment forming the rim of the bowl enclosing the salient. This was the general direction in which we could expect to find the craft, but in broken country this might take several hours. It was hostile territory and the utmost vigilance needed to be applied while keeping up a steady pace employing movement techniques in which the men were well practised, and in which to see intelligently adapted was an education in the use of the terrain. This was done in complete silence without the need for any spoken orders.

After two hours of uninterrupted progress the vanguard section stopped. Moving forward I found to my relief that, in ditching the aircraft, the pilot had, with great skill, brought his machine down in a clearing not far from the track, and so managed the landing as to inflict the minimum damage on the craft and, fortunately, none to himself. As it was he was sitting in the shade of a tree, nonchalantly smoking a cigarette at a safe distance from the machine.

The pilot was a Flight Sergeant. He told me that he had been on a bombing mission but, because of engine trouble, had had to turn back. It was only with great difficulty that he had been able to negotiate the high escarpment. From previous missions he knew of the cart track, and he was able to put his machine down on a relatively even surface resulting in no more damage than a collapsed under-carriage and a bent propellor. While telling me this he expressed concern that the bomb load was still attached to the underside of the wings, and that with the collapse of the fuselage these had become embedded in the soil and could therefore be in a dangerous condition. To avoid risk to the aircraft the bombs needed to be removed, and it was agreed that they be transported to the shade of a tree on the edge of the clearing.

This unwelcome information I transmitted to the Sikh soldiers of my headquarters while the pilot detached the armament. There then came the question as to who was going to 'bell the cat': pick up and carry the first bomb? I looked at my men, and they looked at me. I was able to detect that slight tremor of the muscles of the face with which I was familiar, and which denoted controlled amusement and the message: 'You first, Sahib?' I knew then that there was nothing for it but to pick up one of the bombs and to start walking. After I had covered some yards, feeling uncomfortably conspicuous, I looked round and was not in the least surprised to see the other three bombs being carried by the Sikhs who had, of course, no intention of letting me go it alone.

In the meanwhile close piquetting of the area had been completed, leaving one platoon in reserve. There followed two hours in which nothing could be done except await events in the knowledge that the longer these were delayed the more likely it was that the tribesmen would locate us and mount an attack which might prove difficult to fight off. It was therefore with some relief mingled with astonishment that there arrived along the track from the South a three ton lorry containing a number of aircraftsmen under the command of a technical sergeant accompanied by a large recovery vehicle. The men were unarmed and the small convoy unescorted. This meant that our position was known to higher command, but our predicament not entirely understood since the despatch of so small a body of men through that country without escort was by no means without risk, although it may have had the advantage of surprise: largely mine!

With typical British sangfroid the men dismounted and stood assessing the job to be done. Without comment or orders they unloaded their equipment and at once got to work dismantling the aircraft for loading on the recovery vehicle. At the same time my Sikhs organized a welcome brew up and produced some of their unexpired portions of the previous days rations, which they never travelled without, and which went down well with their RAF guests: good strong vegetable curry and chupattis. Soon they were assisting in the operation and there quickly developed that mutual friendship and cooperation which was always so much a feature of British inter-racial service relations: one of the secrets of Empire.

What next? We were out of touch with any immediate supporting forces. The tribesmen almost certainly knew, at least roughly, where we were, and would be unlikely to pass up an opportunity to secure so valuable a prize as the aircraft, the armament, and indeed the pilot. On the other hand the nature of the terrain was such that their arrival in any force must be delayed for some hours yet. Did we wait to shoot it out in the hope that reinforcements would arrive; or did we make a dash for the post we had come from with cumbersome transport over an indifferent road surface? If we stayed put then a major salvage operation might become necessary against a large body of hostiles: something which the 'powers that be' would hardly welcome, and in any case would take time to lay on. If we took the other alternative then the chances of success were not unreasonable as the tribesmen would be unlikely to know our precise position and strength for so long as we remained mobile.

In assessing the future plans of any tribal fighting force certain limitations on their part needed to be borne in mind. Before committing themselves to any action they would want to know with some accuracy what were their chances of success as regards the size of the opposing force; its constitution; the danger of being surprised; and the existence of a secure getaway in the event of failure. None of these conditions could be satisfied in present circumstances for some time after their arrival; and once they discovered that their opponents were Sikhs of our particular regiment, they would be likely to exercise extra caution.

It was now two o clock in the afternoon. It was estimated that the aircraft would be loaded by five that evening, leaving about two hours daylight in which to cover the distance to the post at about five miles an hour. This was not impossible given fair road conditions. By that time it would be reasonable to expect that some advance elements of a tribal lashkar (fighting force) would be in the vicinity but without the information, or the strength, required to launch an attack which would probably be postponed to the following day by which time, all being well, we would be home and dry.

The decision being made, at five o clock we set off slowly along the track. Our airmen were seated in their vehicles which were preceeded by a small advance party of Sikhs to act as guides and to clear the track of major encumbrances. The remainder of the company were deployed in close formation around the convoy while keeping the surrounding country under surveillance. The light machine guns, one per platoon, were conveniently sited on the recovery vehicle from which height they could give all round protective fire.

Like this we made steady progress until one of those things happened which affect 'the best laid plans' and which tended particularly to occur in frontier operations. During the afternoon it had been noticed that there were heavy thunder storms occurring far away to the west of our position. Owing to the high precipitous nature of the area the accompanying downpour could, and often did, cause severe flooding at a far greater distance from the eye of the storm than might be expected. Thus it was that when we arrived at a point about five miles from the post, where the route lay across a normally dry river bed, we found a torrent of water mixed with earth, rocks, tree trunks, and other impediments rushing down to a depth of some six feet and a width of thirty. There was nothing for it but to stop, close up, and wait for the spate to subside: a matter of two or three hours, and then only if no further storms broke out. At the same time it was getting dark, probably no bad thing in the circumstances.

Whether or not any hostile tribesmen who may have arrived in the area knew of our location, of our intentions, or of our predicament, we had good reason to doubt. But absolute silence and watchfulness needed to be maintained. A few whispered comments emanating from the lorry had to be suppressed by telling its RAF occupants what could happen to their matrimonial prospects if the enemy got in amongst us. So we waited, shivering, after the long hot day in the icy winds which accompanied the water, and every now again checking the flood for any abatement.

After what seemed a very long time the waters began to subside and, as often happens, were reduced to a mere foot or two almost as quickly as they had arrived. It was time to prepare for onward movement when, from my position on the edge of the stream I was able to see against the night sky a body of men carrying rifles and coming towards us over a ridge about one hundred yards ahead and above us. The tension was acute. After a lengthy wait a slight noise from the other side of the stream provoked the whispered question from our side: 'Sok yeh' (pashto - who are you). The answer came: 'Athwanga' (urdu - fifty eighth) the number of the regiment.

We now had under command welcome reinforcements in the form of the Pathan company of our regiment, itself under the command of a highly efficient subedar. As soon as our general situation had become known at regimental headquarters, some twenty miles away, they had been despatched by lorry to the post from where they had at once set out to find us. Their presence made so great a difference to the position that I was tempted to put down anchor and give the tribesmen a bloody nose the next morning. However the object of the exercise was to salvage the aircraft and its personnel, and the possibility of casualties had to be considered.

As it was, I ordered that one platoon of the company be responsible for rear guard protection in case of follow up. Another platoon would act as advanced guard in case of ambush. And the third to clear the track of obstacles including those left behind by the spate which had now left us. It was then a matter of starting up and, in the full glare of the headlights, make steady progress until the post was reached. By this time it was midnight. A problem now arose as to the overnight protection of the aircraft on its bulky recovery vehicle for which there did not seem to be room in the post. This was solved by a highly skilled piece of handling by the RAF driver who managed to steer the load into cover leaving only an inch or two to spare. This left the tribesmen, who had been there alright, to ease their frustration by treating us to some desultory sniping during the night. As was customary, this was ignored.

The next morning our RAF friends who, needless to say, had behaved themselves impeccably throughout what had been a testing adventure, were on their way back to the RAF base along metalled roads through settled territory and under escort by our Pathan company. It was gratifying to witness the broad smiles and hearty handshakes exchanged between the Sikhs and the aircraftsmen pointing to appreciation of each others qualities, neither speaking the other's language.

(b) The Baran River Crossing

Increasingly, as operations on the North West Frontier developed from the intense fighting that took place in the nineteen thirties in the Ipi wars, manoeuvring by night both by small and large formations became a not uncommon practice. This profited from the well known unwillingness on the part of the Pathan tribesman to seriously commit themselves to battle without knowing precisely what the odds were: what size of force they had to contend with; how was it constituted as regards the regiments and armament involved and what are its intentions? In other words, could they fight and run away with fair hope of success and survival, faced as they were with howitzers, machine guns, and aircraft, and often overwhelming superiority in numbers?

In the course of the Ahmadzai operations the element of surprise was frequently and effectively invoked by the Force Commander who believed in keeping the enemy guessing. Thus he would move a lightly equipped Brigade column by night to a selected position deep in the hills from which the guns came within range of many villages which had previously thought themselves secure, and from which infantry units could carry out punitive raids. This required careful planning and training. It had to be admitted that, in spite of the mobility and secrecy the wily tribesman usually had a fair idea of what was up, and in spite of any misgivings would sometimes turn up in force at focal positions from which to monitor the exercise and, if opportunity knocked, to take advantage of any cock-ups.

One fine day, in pursuit of this policy, orders were received for a battalion of the Greyhound Brigade to proceed by night accompanied by a strong contingent of mountain gunners to a location about ten miles distant from the base camp, and there to set up a perimeter camp from which to harass the countryside by carrying the war to the enemy until after a few days withdrawal would take place but this time by a different route, and by daylight so as to inflict casualties on the infuriated tribesmen in hot pursuit. But first there was the business of getting there.

The route, though cross country and not previously negotiated, was relatively simple. It could conveniently be divided into three legs. The first of these ran for about three miles, all the way in the shadow of our friendly moon thrown by a ridge some three hundred feet high. The second leg ran at right angles to the first and provided the only known obstacle in the form of the River Baran which flowed parallel to the initial line of march and which offered a convenient crossing place for the column, also a useful ambush position in the not unlikely presence of any hostiles. Once this obstacle had been cleared then the third leg took off at an angle of forty five degrees across high flat country leading to the proposed camp site.

The column set out at around midnight when the moon was suitably situated to give the necessary cover. Movement was in column of fours to give the maximum control, the maintenance of direction being the responsibility of the 'leading officer' wearing white armlets for identification, who also commanded the forward company which had a scouting and protective role. In this case it was once again the Sikh company of the battalion which would lead the column throughout the operation. As will have been appreciated it was the fording of the river which afforded the most concern and which required a great deal of thought and consideration.

The plan was that on the arrival of the head of the column at the point where by turning left it would arrive within a mile at the crossing point it would halt. The forward company would then become detached from the main body and move independently towards the river. At the proposed fording place this was wider than the rest and therefore shallower, reminiscent of one of John Constable's Suffolk landscapes. A subsidiary nullah housing a small permanent stream led down to the river, and this was covered on both banks by fairly heavy undergrowth. The whole area was commanded by a sugar-loaf hillock some two hundred feet in height, the bolding of which was vital to the crossing. Both banks of the river were high and almost vertical except where a pathway ran down to the shallows. The tasks facing the forward company were threefold.

First, to test the depth of the river at the crossing point, and the firmness of its bottom, as to its suitability for the passage of a large column of men and animals. Second, to find out whether or not the area was manned by hostiles; and third, to clear the area accordingly and secure it until relieved by another company from the main column. The presence of hostile tribesmen had usually to be assumed in any situation offering scope for conflict, and this one was certainly no exception.

To achieve all this with the maximum speed and the minimum casualties the company was divided into three parties. An advance party consisting of the company commander and eight men was to spread out at intervals of a few yards and move slowly and steadily across the river at the crossing point. They were to some extent protected from rifle fire by having behind them the light of the moon which, being particularly bright, presented any marksman with very limited visibility. Also behind them and high up on the near bank was a light machine gun party under the command of a platoon commander whose orders were to open fire forthwith should any shooting commence while the first party would lie down in the water. Such fire was to be directed at all points offering concealment to the enemy, while the third 'attack party' consisting of the remainder of the company would at once move in to clear and secure the area at bayonet point.

In the event no firing took place. All movements took place as directed, except one. The company had been allotted an additional platoon detached from a down-country regiment with, it seemed, little or no frontier experience. Its role in this operation was confined to the occupation and holding of the hillock, and on the completion of the preliminary fording of the river it was despatched for this purpose. All seeming to be well the company commander ran back over the open ground to where the head of the main column was lurking in the shadows and reported 'all clear' whereupon it resumed its march towards the river.

In his later report the company commander admitted that he had been unimpressed with the girth and general unmilitary bearing of the down-country platoon commander, so that it came as no very great surprise but with a great deal of consternation that, on his return to his headquarters, he was confronted by the man surrounded by his men. When asked why he had not carried out his orders by securing the hillock he replied: 'Admi hain' (there are men). It transpired that on his arrival on the position some armed tribesmen, recognising the situation, told him in their own inimitable language to 'push off', and this he had done, taking his men with him. At the same time, in only a minute or two the head of the main column would emerge from the shadows, exposing themselves to concentrated rifle fire causing serious casualties, and possibly bringing the operation to a premature end, matching the career of the company commander.

Something had to be done, and quickly. Accompanied by about a dozen Sikh riflemen who had recognised the situation and needed no orders, the company commander took off up the slope, the party making as much noise as possible on the shale so as to give the impression of a larger force. On reaching the top he was relieved, and the Sikhs no doubt disappointed, to find that the erstwhile occupants had fled: who wouldn't when faced with Sikhs in a hurry! Thus the situation was restored and the operation proceeded as planned. After handing over its protective duties the company continued in its leading role until it reached the end of the third leg exactly on time when another company moved through. That's when the fun started: but that is another story.

(c) A Failed Ambush

One of the many tactical problems facing commanders of units and formations operating on the Frontier in days gone by was the size, strength and siting of outlying picquets designed to protect perimeter camps from heavy sniping or even attack. This was intended to be achieved by the construction and manning of 'sangars', small blockhouses built of stone and earth and sited on high or commanding ground, as far as possible covering approaches to the camp and to the sangars themselves as well as providing protective cross fire to neighbouring picquets.

The Pathan tribesmen were adept at assessing their chances of success in attacking and sometimes seizing such strongholds. Moving swiftly and silently in small groups, wearing grass chapplis, and carrying long knives, they would concentrate their force at a point near to the picquet from which they would launch their attack. This was accompanied by a great deal of noise: shouts and yells as they attempted to breach the defences in the face of the use of hand-grenades, bayonets, and sometimes the dreaded kukri.

Not long after the Ahmadzai Force had established its base inside the perimeter of the Salient word came through the intelligence grape vine not only that an attack was planned against one of the picquets, but also giving the date and time this was due to take place. Owing to the nature of the terrain the picquet under threat was sited too far from the camp to be adequately supported; on the other hand to leave the position undefended was unthinkable. Orders were therefore received that counter-steps should be taken to intercept. This meant a night ambush: and the Sikh company would carry it out.

As will be seen, not for the last time in the course of these operations did a friendly moon and the shadows it cast have an influence on events. Seen from the shelter of the targetted picquet it was clear that there was only one valid approach available to the attackers and that was a well defined nullah leading up to the foot of the hill on which the picquet stood. Some two hundred yards short of this a secondary nullah formed a junction with the main approach and it was here that, at the anticipated time, it was calculated that the bright moonlight would give way to heavy shadows thus enabling the attacking force to form up and proceed under cover of virtual darkness. It was here also that the ambush would be laid.

Conveniently situated between the picquet and the camp there was a large banyan tree. This provided a base from which two platoons would proceed to their battle positions, while leaving one platoon in reserve under command of the Sikh subadar 2 i/c. It would also provide a collecting point after completion of the operation and a link with the camp. Of the 'sharp-end' platoons only one section would form part of the ambush party, the remainder consisting of the company commander, his escort and staff, and three light machine guns consolidated under the control of a platoon commander.

The ambush party, consisting of some ten men including the commander, would take up a position on slightly raised ground overlooking but laid back from the nullah junction; the machine gun party being sited on a piece of commanding ground about fifty yards on the picquet side of the main nullah which jinked conveniently at that point to give a good field of fire. The remainder of the two platoons would take up positions covering the secondary nullah and to the rear of the ambush party so as to deal with any outflanking move or anything unforeseen: always a factor.

The operation was to be sparked off as and when a sufficient concentration of tribesmen were calculated to be at the ambush point whereupon the commander would lob in a grenade. The explosion would be immediately followed by concentrated fire aimed straight up the nullah by the machine guns until terminated by a long blast on a whistle when the whole party would move slowly and quietly back to the banyan tree, each section reporting as it arrived.

All these plans having been exhaustively explained to the men the time came when, at around midnight and in the receding shadow of the moon, positions had been taken up and all that was missing was the presence of the attacking force. There was not long to wait. Although not a sound had been heard by the ambush party coming from the nullah below, a large stone, clearly propelled by human hand, landed with a thump among the watchers. This was an old trick employed by tribesmen as a means of discovering the presence or otherwise of any enemy, and it would have been ignored at that point. As it was, one of the younger members of the ambush party, unable to restrain his zeal, lifted his bearded face over the lip of the nullah and thus clearly visible against the night sky, there was a scuffle from below, and that was 'it'.

Not unexpectedly the tribesmen had despatched a small advance party to do what they had done while a substantial main body remained in wait. The question remained that although the planned attack on the picquet must now be 'off', had they any reserve plans such as the counter-ambush of the company on its way back to camp? The immediate need was to withdraw forthwith to the collecting point, thus approaching the camp from a different angle and the necessary signals were given. But all was not over.

On arrival at the banyan tree the commander was horrified to be informed that one of the sections had not reported and was overdue. It seemed unlikely that they could have been ambushed and butchered without sound. There was a possibility that they might have failed to receive the withdrawal order and might therefore still be in their action positions. Something had to be done and a section, led in person by the commander, set out along a subsidiary ravine, still concealed by shadow, until it made junction with the principal watercourse. From this point all was revealed in the bright moonlight in the form of two young tribesmen sitting together on the edge of the ravine with their legs dangling over the side at a distance of about two hundred yards, and with their rifles over their knees.

It was apparent that no action could have taken place nor be intended. This was confirmed on return to the tree when the commander was informed that the section commander had mistaken his orders and led his party straight back to camp at considerable risk and to the fury of everyone.

(d) The Storming of the Grang

In order to open up and control for all time the movements of the Wazir tribesmen intent on committing one mischief or another against the safe background of a hitherto impenetrable bolt-hole, the principal objective of the Ahmadzai operations was the seizing and securing of the Grang feature. This lay at the end of a vast mountainous area situated in the centre of the Salient and stretching some ten miles or so until culminating in a huge massif, shaped like a ruined mediaeval castle, and dominating the environment for many miles around. This was known as Bannu Castle.

The importance of the Grang to the Ahmadzai Force consisted in the fact that from its position there led down into the plain below a long relatively gentle spur giving scope for the construction of a metalled road up a reasonable gradient to a strongly fortified constabulary post to be sited at the summit of the ridge. From here all the way to the Castle the face of the terrain was cliff-like, tall and precipitous, and, at first sight from the front at least, impassable, rising almost sheer to a height of some one thousand feet from the plain: in some places more. Once the road had reached the ridge there was little by way of technical obstacle to prevent its progress onwards across the remainder of the country until arrival in settled territory.

For those concerned in the seizing and holding of this key area the prospect posed a tactical problem similar to that encountered by Sir William Lockhart when faced with the need to capture and control the Samana Ridge at the commencement of the Tirah campaign in 1897. Historians will remember that the operations commenced with the British assault on the Dargai Heights and the capture of a village of that name which provided the key to further advance into the Tirah, home of the Afridis and the Orakzais considered to be the fiercest fighting men in the world, and the best marksmen in Asia.

The line of attack to the village lay up a bare slope some three hundred yards in length and offering little cover from the murderous fire rained down on the advancing troops by several thousand determined and well concealed tribesmen. Casualties mounted steeply, and for five hours the British assault force, consisting of the 2nd Gurkhas, the Derbyshires and the Dorsets endeavoured to reach their objective only to be thwarted by the unsuitability of the terrain and the resistance of the tribesmen. Reinforcements were sent in: the Gordon Highlanders and the 3rd Sikhs. The former, by an heroic charge spurred on by the playing of 'Cock o' the North' by Piper Findlater of the Gordons who, although shot through both legs, continued to play until the position was taken and the tribesmen fled. He was awarded the Victoria Cross.

Those now planning a similar assault on the Grang were faced with what at first sight seemed the need to negotiate a bare slope of the same length and lack of cover to that encountered at Dargai forty four years before, and in the face of a reported substantial buildup of a tribal force well suited to resist by fire. The orders were to advance up the spur, only one company to be employed as a spearhead, others to follow as the situation required. But long experience of frontier tactical conditions caused the leading company commander, after close reconnaissance of the area through field glasses and a prolonged scrutiny of air photographs, to question the advisability of that line of advance.

What this careful search of the terrain revealed was that immediately to the right of the spur there was a steep re-entrant which, though seemingly impassible, led to the top. If able to be negotiated this approach had the very great advantage of being defiladed on either side by outcrops of rock leaving an area of some fifty yards in between up which fit and determined men could scramble, protected from the flanks and out of sight of the enemy, until reaching the summit and a protective ridge behind which the company could form up for the final assault.

What the photographs also revealed was that immediately over the ridge there were deep chasms on either side of a natural bridge some thirty yards wide by fifty yards long offering the attackers the only passage on to more open terrain from which the four platoons involved could debouch. It also offered the tribesmen a convenient killing ground as only a limited number of the assault force could pass over the bridge at any given time. The plan was for the first platoon across immediately to turn right and make its way up a tall feature to be known as 'Top' which dominated the surrounding countryside. A second platoon would follow in close support. It was around this feature that the tribesmen could be expected to be entrenched as there was plenty of defensive cover against any artillery or machine gun supporting fire from the plain below.

Immediately ahead of the bridge and at a distance of about three hundred yards there was a secondary ridge leading to a pinnacle of what was little more than a rocky outcrop but which provided cover for snipers or small bodies of tribesmen intent on mischief. As will be seen it was a tactical nuisance. On the far side the land fell away steeply to descend into the main valley. It was here, that company headquarters would be set up under the protection of a third platoon, while a fourth platoon, 'borrowed' from another company, would hold the bridgehead and act as general reserve.

These plans having been approved, with difficulty, by higher command, it fell to the Sikh company to carry them out. The virtual scaling of the heights was carried out with precision and at a speed to cause astonishment among the onlookers from below, the Sikhs enhancing their vigor by the consumption of coriander seeds. There was a short pause under the ridge while all the platoons closed up. This done and, on a short blast of the commander's whistle, he and his subedar 2 i/c broke cover and, followed by others of his headquarters, dashed over the bridge expecting to be greeted by a volley of musketry. Nothing happened, and the company deployed according to orders so that in the shortest time the position was secure.

From later intelligence reports it seemed that the tribesmen had indeed been present and in position in some force expecting the assault to be launched up the spur, and not by the chosen route which they considered impossible. Thus they remained oblivious of the situation until the assaulting force was concentrated only a short distance from their positions whereupon, true to form, they faded away, treating themselves to a few parting sniper shots from a safe distance. As it was therefore the only reception to be received by the commander came from an old nanny goat who greeted him in the usual way. He later admitted that his frustration at the non-consummation of his plans tempted him to shoot the animal between the eyes, but that the 'love at first sight' look on its face saved its life.

(e) The Defence of the Grang Picquets

It was too much to expect that men as intractable as the Mehauds and Wazirs would be content to allow what has been a tactical defeat to go unpunished. Their failure to achieve some success would have given rise to much mockery the whole length of the frontier. It was therefore in anticipation of some counter stroke, even possibly aimed at recovery of the Grang position, that orders were given for the immediate construction of a network of picquets, well-fortified and manned so as to prevent any reoccupation of the area by the tribesmen. At the same time protective cover would be provided to the daily working parties carrying out constructional work on the road and other projects.

Notwithstanding that the Sikh company, in carrying out the successful assault might have been thought to have done their fair share, they were ordered first to site and build the picquets, and then to man them for five days and nights. Being at a distance of some two miles from the base camp there was no prospect of any realistic fire support so that they could be exposed to serious attack, mainly by night. The defensive layout therefore needed careful planning.

The plans included the erection of four sangars, each to be manned by a platoon and strongly fortified by two aprons of barbed wire and other impediments. Each platoon had its own light machine gun and an ample supply of grenades: essential to this form of defence. All round defence and inter picquet support were needed, particularly covering the main approaches along which sudden attacks could be launched. In our previous subchapter the features 'Pimple' and 'Top' have been mentioned. The existence, shape, size and location of the former gave rise to the problem of how it could be neutralised so as to prevent its occupation by attacking tribesmen and the resulting plunging fire which might well provide the corner stone to any attack. There was no room on 'Pimple' for the siting of a viable picquet; and 'Top' was a normally unacceptable distance from the main cluster.

The three other picquets were sited around, and at a distance of about one hundred yards from Pimple. First there was the command picquet housing a platoon with its light machine gun, company headquarters, and a heavy machine gun section with two principal roles: to put down supporting defensive fire in aid of Top, if attacked; and to cover Pimple with concentrated prophylactic fire should it be occupied by tribesmen. For either one of these needs raised platforms were built inside the picquet. The other two picquets were situated to the north and south of Pimple respectively, each one covering the rear of the feature while remaining in full view of the Headquarters picquet. All were connected by field telephone and all were strongly fortified. By the end of the day a substantial and probably secure redoubt had been established.

Having been left by the Bridge to follow its own fortunes the company settled down to await events. Each day the area was visited by working parties and their protective covers as the alignment of the new road was dug, water tanks installed, and heavy telephone poles manhandled up the hill. Their presence enabled the Sikhs to relax and recover the sleep which was denied to them at nighttime owing to the doubling of the sentry duties.

For the first three nights there were no developments. The fourth day broke with that look in the sky, and feeling on the breeze which pressaged bad weather. By late afternoon rumbles of distant thunder and flashes of lightning could be heard and seen. This came ominously nearer until shortly after nightfall the storm broke with a sudden vigor and the sky was lit up by almost continuous flashes of lightning followed by shattering crashes of thunder, while the rain fell in sheets.

Not long before this sounds of heavy firing had been heard from the direction of the camp. Whether or not this was intended as a distraction in aid of the main purpose which was to launch an attack in force on the Grang picquets is not known, but the fact is that about an hour later, at around midnight, with the storm showing no sign of abatement, heavy and accurate rifle fire directed at the northern picquet broke out from the shelter of Pimple. Here it seemed that a substantial body of tribesmen were concentrated, having climbed up the steep and watery slope from the valley below, presumably with the intention of neutralising the picquet by fire while scaling Pimple in sufficient numbers to command the two remaining picquets.

To circumvent this the heavy machine gun in the Headquarters picquet, sited primarily in support of Top but with a secondary role to provide for such a situation as this, was moved to cover Pimple and if needed to fire indiscriminately, thereby coming as a nasty surprise to the attackers. But this did not have to happen.

In the days before World War Two mortars were not available for use in Frontier fighting. Had they been they would have been invaluable. Much use was made of the hand grenade in close combat; and occasionally of the rifle grenade, a clumsy device consisting of a specially adapted service rifle capable of throwing a hand grenade up to one hundred and fifty yards from a cup fitted to the end of the muzzle. A good deal of willed manipulation was needed accurately to adjust the range, and care had to be taken to ensure against any obstacles on the flight path which might cause the projectile to fall short and hoist the operator with his own petard.

To launch the grenade a special propellant cartridge was inserted in the breach of the rifle. The operator would then sit down on the ground on which he would rest the rifle butt while pointing the weapon in the required direction. He would then press the trigger with his forefinger while keeping the rest of his hand away from the mechanism to avoid damage from the recoil. As the grenade left the cup the safety lever would be released, the projectile would sail through the air, and seven seconds later (sometimes three) a highly efficient explosion would take place, hopefully on target. When all this takes place by day it has to be treated with considerable caution; by night in dark and tempestuous conditions it requires a great deal of skill and courage.

Exhibiting that quiet professionalism which is characteristic of the Indian soldier, a Sikh naik (corporal), ignoring the hail of bullets being poured on the picquet, sat down calmly on the flooded ground and after systematically carrying out the preliminaries let fly the projectile which, precisely as planned, landed with a shattering explosion on the reverse side of Pimple, exactly where the tribesmen must have been collected. This was followed at short intervals by two more of the same after which there was silence except for the now fading thunderclaps and the sound of rain water rushing down the mountain side and carrying with it stones and other natural debris.

After one hour during which all picquets stood to in case of further developments it became apparent that this quite unexpected 'tour de force' had effectively put an end to the tribesmens' ambitions. A dawn search of the area revealed a sufficient number of spent cartridge cases to indicate the presence of a strong body of men and therefore no mere sniping expedition. At the same time the heavy rain had washed out any traces of casualties as there must have been.

To end this tale of derring do on a human note mention is made of Ban Banai. He was an old Wazir tribesman who had been recovered by patrol carrying out a search of a village situated some distance from and below the picquet area. Owing to his great age and frailty he had had to be abandoned by the villagers who had fled into the hills on the advance of troops into the area. He was carried up to Headquarters picquet like a heap of rags on a charpoi with little to protect him from the chill wind that was then blowing. He was quickly covered over by spare blankets, but when the Sikh subedar offered him a mug of hot sweet tea he brushed it aside angrily. It turned out that he remembered the time when the Sikhs Army, commanded by their famous General, Hari Singh, had sent soldiers into the village to seize six of the younger tribesmen whom they summarily shot in reprisal for some peccadillo or another: Banai and others having taken to the hills.

On the evidence of this information, and after further detailed interrogation, it transpired that the old gentleman was some one hundred and thirty six years old. Apart from his huge bald head, with its prominent hooked nose and alert blue eyes, his body had shrunk so that his atrophied muscles hung loosely from the bones of arms and legs, the skin being mottled and discoloured.

Four years later, at the end of WW2, enquiries were made as to the fate of this phenomenon. It seemed that he was alive and well and living with relatives in the Punjab. How old can you get!

(f) A Gallant Charger

The Ahmadzai campaign having been brought to a satisfactory conclusion, all aims having been accomplished, the captains and kings departed, leaving the fighting columns to disperse according to their destinations and means of transport. These included the Kohat contingent of which a marching column consisting of an escorting company; a battery of mountain gunners; and a large body of odds and sods carrying a variety of military impedimenta on strings of mules.

This column had orders to march the seventy miles from Bannu to Kohat by road across reputedly peaceful country, although the route was parallel to and not far from the Salient boundary and was therefore always prone to attack. By now it was late May and the daytime heat was intense so that even if unmolested the march was to be no picnic. The first stage of some fifteen miles led to a large constabulary post situated on the edge of the Latambar nala. The area of the post had been expanded to provide a semi-fortified permanent perimeter camp for the accommodation of large bodies of troops 'en passage'.

The environment was true desert. No birds or flowers and only a few pepper trees existed to lighten its grim prospect. The nala itself was fed by a veritable maze of minor ravines giving valuable cover to any badmashes operating in the area as they not infrequently did. As it was the local tribesmen were now busy licking their wounds and seeking to repair their bruised izzat (pride) resulting from their defeat. They let it be known that they intended to exact retribution from the column. A sort of

Parthian shot. This came as good news to the ever-belligerent Sikhs whose company was to provide the escort.

To the company commander who must command the column, and who, according to intelligence reports, had been singled out by name for special attention by the tribesmen, feelings were mixed. It was one thing to command a fully trained and disciplined body of men taking part in whatever form of action as might present itself; but another thing altogether to have responsibility for the safety of a large number of non-combatants, mule leaders and the like, spread back over a long and vulnerable line of march.

The lie of the land was such that only some ten miles of the route offered any real opportunity to any miscreants wanting to attack or impede the column. The first part of this was the Latambar nala itself, the crossing of which was essential, and which was wide open to sniping attacks from the shelter of the many minor ravines which criss-crossed the area to the west and offered convenient getaways through the main tangi. The second part consisted of some five miles of roadway passing through precipitous hilly country of typical frontier character along which all traffic had to pass, and which had been the scene of bloody ambushes and other encounters in the past. Indeed for several years no passage was permitted except between certain hours on fixed days of the week when the route would be piquetted by troops based on Latambar camp.

This was the setting against which the column commander had to make his plan whereby to bring his protégés safely past the danger points. But once more, as so often in war, the 'best laid plans...' As we know the Latambar nala ran east to west until it disappeared into the rugged hills of the salient. To the east, and to the right of the line of advance, the country was wide open and flat offering no cause for concern. Nevertheless one of two armoured cars which had been allotted to the company was positioned on some conveniently high ground, thus providing a protective picquet on that flank.

On the more vulnerable western flank a platoon of Sikhs was posted to picquet the approaches on either side of the nala at a distance of some three hundred yards from the crossing place, and this was supported by a second armoured car. At the same time a second platoon was despatched across the nala to search the road for explosives, to secure the opposite bank, and to clear the camp. The rest of the force, including the ubiquitous gunners, were closed up in a spacious cutting giving access to the floor of the nala while awaiting orders to move forward.

These precautionary dispositions having been completed the moment came for the main body to commence the crossing. This was led by the mule convoy consisting of strings of three mules each, many of them carrying small arms ammunition and led by sepoys of the Service Corps. As the first string set off the column commander mounted his charger so as to have maximum mobility in the event of incident. The horse was a fine well-disciplined animal which had served his master faithfully and well over several years. He was well known and much admired, indeed coveted by many, attracting a great deal of affection among the troops who labelled him 'Pink Nose' because that is what he possessed.

The first string of mules, accompanied about five yards to the right by the mounted commander, had covered only a short distance in the nala when there was a shattering explosion. According to the commander's later report this is what happened:

'I had been uneasily aware that if any kind of attack was to come it would be here and soon. The explosion came from the leading mule which was blown to pieces as a multicoloured sheet of flame seemingly bounced on the road before bursting into the air above. I had just time to witness this before I received a violent blow on the side of the forehead which knocked me semi-conscious. I came to on hearing a squeal of pain from Pink Nose who had lost part of his famous nose to a piece of shrapnel and, with the blast, had sat down on the tarmac only to get up smartly from the effect being akin to sitting in a pan full of hot oil.

By dint of hanging on instinctively to the horse's mane and to the saddle accoutrements I found myself still in situ when the equilibrium had been restored. There was blood everywhere: some of it came from the mule, some from the horse, and a lot from me as it streamed down my face and all over my shirt from a small but highly productive wound high up on my head.

Remarkably the horse, though trembling all over from the shock, had, against his natural instincts, stood his ground. Many, perhaps most, would have bolted in terror at the sight and smell of blood, the noise and stench of explosive, the pain from his wounded nose and scalded rump, and the remains of the mule still kicking its life out on the ground, while the mule leader and the two other animals in the string remained untouched, the former still astonishingly holding on to the lead rope. Had he bolted he might have carried me out of control into the hands of the enemy to be butchered in a manner well known to and practised by Pathan tribesmen. The fact that he did not was very greatly to his credit and a tribute to his intelligence and courage, his only thought being the safety of his rider: or so it seemed.'

After taking stock it transpired that a whole box of some fifty primed hand grenades being carried on the mule had 'gone up'. The established cause was a bullet fired from a modern service rifle, and it clearly came from a position some six hundred yards along the western end of the nala from where the column was debouching. It was safe to assume that the shot was aimed specifically at the column commander, conspicuous on his charger, as the direction was perfect. Had the sniper taken proper account of the fact that, as every Bisley marksman knows, when there is a severe heat haze as indeed there was at the time, then firing from a range of six hundred yards the sights on a rifle need to be adjusted upwards by at least one hundred yards. Failing this the bullet will fall short, which it did at the expense of one poor mule.

The immediate problem arising out of the explosion was the wide distribution of grenades in every stage of dangerous delapidation in and on either side of the road. This required the commander and several experienced NCOs to spend some two hours in the afternoon sun: first, finding and marking the location of each weapon; then segregating them with sandbags to lessen the effect of any premature explosion; and finally de-detonating them before destroying them with small charges. While this was going on the entire company had to remain at 'red alert' in case of attack.

It was only when the column commander was able temporarily to relax in camp that he realised what it was to suffer from severe shock so that the prospect of continuing the march for another fifteen miles on the following day, with the likelihood of having to fight some sort of action on the way, caused him considerable consternation. The tribesmen, having witnessed the explosion, would have their tails up with the expectation that there had been casualties, probably including the British commander, and were therefore unlikely to forego the opportunity of repeating what they saw as a success by putting up strong opposition to the next stage of the march in country favourable to such plans.

It was here that the ever-solicitous and imaginative Subadar 2 i/c of the company came forward with typical Sikh pragmatism. Why not complete the next stage by night: breaking camp after the evening meal and moving in complete silence while leaving the cooking fires alight to deceive the inevitable watchers? Thus the five hour march moving in column could be over by two or three in the morning without the knowledge of the tribesmen who, according to their custom, would be unlikely to be in position for the encounter before dawn. After the gruelling day which had just passed, both men and animals would welcome the cool air of the night and the freedom from threat.

And so it was. Each well-drilled section, after making sure that all metal parts of equipment were cushioned against noise, slipped out quietly on to the road and moved off in close column with bayonets fixed. Pink Nose was spared the need to carry his master whose condition was now such that contrary to custom he was forced to ride, but on a borrowed horse while Pink Nose followed behind looking, it was thought, a trifle stuffy as he was led by his sais (groom). Thus in good order and no little relief the column arrived before dawn at Bahadur Khel, an old Sikh fort which marked the end of the hazardous area.

Suddenly there came a hustle and a bustle as the General arrived in his staff car. He ordered the column commander into the vehicle and sped him off to hospital in Kohat. X-rays and other investigations revealed that three minute particles of metal had presumably passed through the dead mule, thus cushioning their impact, and lodged in the officer's cranium (where they remain to this day), but that in spite of the small size of the wound a lot of blood had been lost. But nothing that a month's leave in the fleshpots could fail to remedy.

(g) The DIY Tribesman

It was sometime after the aircraft incident that the occupation of the Ahmadzai Salient was planned to commence. As already mentioned the principal ground forces consisted of two highly trained and experienced Brigades supported by air and artillery: mainly mountain batteries capable of negotiating the most exacting terrain at high speed, and of bringing down accurate fire where and when wanted. This required the skilled handling of huge mules carrying the stocks and barrels of the 3.7 howitzers then in use, by huge men capable of bringing the equipment into action in a remarkably short time. This brought welcome assistance or relief to hard pressed riflemen making their way under fire high on any hillside.

From the plains around Bannu, the base for the operations, there were two main entrances to the Salient, both of them by way of passes through steep and rugged defiles giving plenty of scope for concealment and resistance to defending tribesmen. Kohat Brigade, which came to be known as 'Barstow's

Greyhounds' because of its highly mobile role, had the task of forcing the Latamber Pass (or Tangi) and probing into the hills beyond, thus harassing the rear of the defenders of the Gumatti Tangi further south which was to be the target of Bannu Brigade.

On the appointed day the Brigade column left camp in the early hours so that, by daybreak the battalion were drawn up on each side of the line of advance, ready to storm the lofty and precipitous heights forming the flanks of the nala. It was early February when even the austere surroundings showed up at their best in the early morning sun. An air of anticipation filled the atmosphere as the signal to advance was awaited. This was encouraged by the sound of 'noises off' emanating from the Gumatti Tangi where stiff resistance appeared to have been encountered. All eyes were therefore focussed on the crests of the hills where similar resistance might be expected to materialise. Then, as so often in frontier operations, something altogether unexpected happened.

Over the skyline on the left hand side of the tangi there appeared a solitary figure. It was a tall young tribesman who stood for half a minute before swaggering down the hill towards us. The tails of his shirt and puggaree fluttered in the early morning breeze. Over his shoulder he sported an old muzzle-loading jezail. Stopping at the lip of a vertical cliff, about six hundred feet above us, he shaded his eyes against the sun. One recalled the lines of Kipling:

> He trod the ling,
> Like a buck in Spring
> and he looked like a lance in rest.

As he stood, gazing out across the plain beneath him, he was seen suddenly to start. He had suddenly become aware that an entire brigade of ill-intentioned soldiers was drawn up at his feet as if for his inspection. Many in his place would have wasted no time in beating a hasty retreat back across the skyline whence he had come: but not he.

Unslinging his old musket, he sat down on a convenient boulder and proceeded systematically to load and prime the weapon with the crude ammunition normally used. This usually consisted of a three or four inch nail coated with soft lead filled with broken razor blades, tin tacks, bits of glass, and anything else calculated to inflict serious damage on hitting flesh.

All being ready he cocked up the muzzle to give maximum range and, amid clouds of smoke, let fly. This he repeated several times in different directions, no doubt so as to ensure that everyone got a fair share. The projectiles advertised their passing by emitting that sinister whistling sound with which most veteran frontier soldiers will be familiar. "The flying bullet down the Pass, that whistles clear: All flesh is grass" (Kipling).

Although the presence of this interloper posed no serious threat to anyone, it constituted an embarrassment. How was he to be removed and by whom? To pick him off at that range with sun and wind to contend with would be not only difficult but unsporting: like shooting a sitting bird. The answer came from the rear when a lordly voice rang out: 'Leave 'im to the Gunnars', and in a remarkably short time a howitzer shell landed some yards to the man's left. He took not the slightest notice as others arrived but continued with his self-allotted defensive role until, his ammunition exhausted, he stood up, reslung his old bandhook and, turning, sauntered back up the hill. On reaching the crest he paused and looked back before descending on the other side. It is fair to comment that had he been better educated he might have taken his leave with the use of a certain Churchillian gesture.

Chapter Nine
India: Shikar

In chapter 6 mention was made of the three subjects of conversation the most frequently to be heard in an Indian Army Officers' Mess, namely: sex, shop and shikar. In a country as rich in life as was the Indian sub-continent in those earlier times, giving opportunities to all so inclined to indulge relatively inexpensively in the pursuit of game of all varieties, the scope for the exchange of experiences was wide enough to take the place of more mundane subjects.

All over India and Burma were to be found wild animals of many different species. But understandably the better specimens were only to be found in the underpopulated and less accessible places requiring long approach marches, and much organisational 'bandobast' which all formed part of an officer's training in how to make the best use of scarce resources. This had the beneficial effect for both hunted and hunter of restricting the sport to responsible enthusiasts with an interest in conservation, and not in slaughter for the sake of it.

In shooting such game the purpose was generally to mark down, stalk and kill cleanly as fine a specimen as could be found of any particular breed. But while roaming forest plain or hillside in search of such trophies the sportsman would be witness to many events, great and small, which would enrich his experience and thus cement his attachment to a life so full of opportunity for the study of nature at its wildest. Indeed those bitten with this sort of enthusiasm would, when their turn came for leave, time and again eschew the fleshpots of Kashmir and sundry hill stations for the high hills, the deep jungles, and the broad plains where game abounded.

A Christmas holiday spent in camp in the forests of the United or Central Provinces when the air was like champagne, and each morning was greeted by jungle cries of the denizens: peacocks, jungle fowl, parrots and a myriad of songbirds, also the chattering of monkeys, was sheer delight and rich reward to those so much of whose life had to be spent in less amenable places and climates. A march through the jungle armed with a shot gun or a .22 rifle for shooting a pea or jungle fowl for the pot, followed by a gun bearer carrying a heavier weapon in case of need, would be a stimulating experience.

The need for conservation of many species of game in India was recognised in the time of the Raj from early times by the introduction of various systems of licensing, not always altogether effective in preventing the unlawful killing and selling for profit of wild animals for their hides, heads, or meat. While the shooting of many species of game has continued to be subject to controls according to need, political changes often resulting in a failure of law and order may have had their effect on the availability of good sport such as our early predecessors enjoyed. The nature of that sport which was regarded as one of the chief compensations for exile in India can to some extent be assessed from the following short descriptions of the principal participants, namely the horned sheep, deer and antelope.

Leaving aside for the time being the more dangerous species of game: tigers, leopards, bison and bear, we may now examine the scope which exists all over India for the hunting of the more common breeds of wild animal. Starting in the far North we find herds of Oorial which is described as 'a sturdily built wild sheep of light foxy red colour standing about thirty two inches at the shoulder, with curved corrugated horns about thirty inches long'. It is normally located in the hills of the Northern Punjab and the Frontier Province, and was at one time considered to provide the best and most accessible sport available.

Similarly located but a great deal more difficult of access is the Markhor which varies in size, colouration and shape of horns, according to its habitat. Generally it is of larger build than the Oorial with horns varying from the straight spiralled cork-screw-like effect about thirty inches long, to the more divergent less elegant type running up to about fifty inches round the curves. This used to be a much poached animal in spite of its evasive abilities which, together with other characteristics, have earned it the reputation as 'king of hill game'.

Once described as 'the finest big game field of the world' with particular emphasis on the splendour of climate and scenery, Kashmir offers to the sportsman a huge variety of game situated in challenging locations, although access must now be seriously limited by political problems. In earlier times, and probably still, most shooting had to be done under licence with strict limits on the number of heads to be allowed. The 'bag' might include the Kashmir Stag, known as Barasingh, more or less confined to the province. This fine beast stands about fifty two inches at the shoulder, with length of antlers up to fifty inches, the normal number of points being five but can go up to twelve or fourteen. It can be found in forested areas at nine thousand feet or more.

Also in Kashmir are to be found the Markhor, the Oorial, the Himalayan Goural: a smallish goat with up to eight inch horns, and various antelopes and gazelles including the Blackbuck. Moving up higher in the mountains there are herds of the spectacular Ibex, stoutly built animals of the goat species weighing some two hundred pounds with heavy corrugated horns sweeping back in a long curve to a length of up to fifty inches the points almost touching their backs. Their normal place of abode lies in rocky outcrops at around twelve thousand feet where they add conveniently to the diet of the equally remote long tailed snow leopard. At this height also may be found the Himalayan Brown Bear, known also as the Red Bear, and the Serow, once described as 'a clumsy mixture of donkey, goat, and antelope' with horns about nine inches long in a slight curve. Difficult to shoot owing to their skilful use of ground. Finally there is the Bharal, with curved and twisted horns measuring about twenty five inches. This animal lives in large herds at sixteen thousand feet in summer, probably the highest and most exhilarating to hunt of all Kashmiri goats.

Worthy of special mention among high altitude mountain sheep is the Himalayan Tahr: a fine animal weighing about one hundred and eighty pounds, and standing about thirty eight inches at the shoulder. A good set of horns would be about fourteen inches in length, and a particular and attractive feature is the long fine flowing hair with which the animal is covered. They are 'hard to get' as they inhabit difficult ground: high cliffs, rocks, and forests, and have a good head for heights. This being so they probably remain pretty numerous being distributed all the way down the Himalayan foothills.

As an illustration of the ruggedness of character of this noble beast, and of the rich experience so often gained by the sportsman in India, the author was sitting on the steep side of a green valley at about nine thousand feet in the Himalayas when, through his binoculars he spotted a female Tahr standing far up on the exposed face of the sheer cliff over a drop of many hundreds of feet on the other side. Between its forelegs there stood a small kid, and this had attracted the attention of a huge eagle with a wing span of some twelve feet which was carrying out determined attacks in an endeavour to seize the little animal, only to be repulsed over and over again by the short but sharp horns of the mother, weilded with great determination. After a number of fierce passes the marauding bird gave up end then, apparently in exasperated search for other prey, glided gracefully down the valley, hardly moving its massive wings as it made use of the air currents, and passing within about two hundred yards, and at about the same level, as the onlooker.

Moving southwards from Kashmir and the Punjab into the rich fields of Central India the sportsman is rewarded with a wide choice of areas where game abounds in spite of steady depletion resulting over many years from poaching, and the difficulty of applying controls in so large and varied a country. Nevertheless one assumes that game is still plentiful offering enjoyment to those seeking fine trophies or, perhaps more usual today, exercising photographic skills. Probably the most representative of these area has at all times been the United and Central Provinces with their good road and rail facilities, and the variety of terrain ranging from wide open plains, vast forests, and hill country, suitable as habitat for many different species. It is here also that the more dangerous game animals are to be found. However, concentrating for the time being on deer and antelope the whole of India offers plenty of scope for the tracking down of such species es the Sambhar, the Chital, Swamp Deer, Blackbuck, Chinkara, and the Four-Horned Antelope: to mention only a few of the more prominent.

The two most widely distributed deer to be found throughout the Indian sub-continent are the Sambhar and the Chital, or Spotted Deer. The Sambhar varies in size as one proceeds southwards from fifty two inches in the north to about fifty five in central locations. Their preferred habitat is in hilly regions: they have been seen at up to nine thousand feet. Good horns would measure up to thirty five inches in southerly areas, more further north. The stags are pugnacious animals, having developed a fiercely aggressive style by reason of its many enemies such as man, tigers, and leopards. They have been known to kill men when pressed or cornered. They are difficult to approach, having good hearing and noses, though poor eyesight, making for good sport.

The Chital is a particularly beautiful animal. Very gracefully built it bears a light chestnut coat freshly spotted with white. The horns are usually six-pointed and about thirty five inches long. They may be found in open forest and grassy plains and are therefore relatively easy to shoot, moving in herds of around fifty but often considerably more. A fine target for the photographer. This account provides outline details of only a few of the better known, and more often encountered, horned and antlered goats and deer. Other animals such as the Swamp Deer, the Barking Deer, the Mouse Deer, the Wild Pig, the Chitah, the Striped Hyena, the wild Dog, the Lynx, all contribute to the natural wealth of the sub-continent, as do the more dangerous species which we will now discuss.

It was frequently the ultimate aim of the sportsman to 'bag a tiger'. These fine animals could be found throughout India south of Kashmir and the Rajputana desert. Before embarking on such an enterprise it was necessary, in the days of the Raj, to obtain a licence to shoot and the use of a 'block' with limits on the amount of game permitted to be shot. Many arrangements needed to be made whereby to attract the tiger to where it could be shot, and then to secure a clean kill so as not to be faced with the perilous task of following up a wounded and therefore angry beast well capable of turning the tables by hunting and destroying the hunter.

Most people have seen tigers in captivity or on screens or will have read about them and will accordingly be aware of the size, shape and characteristics of the animal. A really good specimen trophy might yield a skin measuring as much as ten feet between pegs with an additional five inches or so over curves. They probably enjoy a life span of some twenty five years feeding largely on sambhar and cheetal. Sadly in recent years they have become an endangered species owing partly to the alleged medical properties of certain parts and to the difficulties of controlling widespread poaching arising from the considerable commercial profits to be made.

There are several ways of hunting tigers, the most common being 'sitting up' over bait, dead or alive. This involves the secure fastening of a chair or other form of seating in a tree over looking a clearing where the bait can be situated, preferably near to water, and the tethering of a live buffalo in the hope that the tiger will be tempted to kill it and be shot in the process, usually by night. Another way is to encourage local inhabitants to bring news of any 'kill' which has occurred and to which the tiger will certainly return if there is anything left to eat. The same practices would apply where the target is a leopard, but probably with a smaller bait, such as a goat.

Experienced hunters often favour the digging of a 'boma' at ground level overlooking the killing ground and protected from attack, by tough thorn bushes. A powerful torch is necessary to be switched on as soon as noises indicate that the animal is on the kill, the hunter being in the lying position with rifle at the ready. This method is adopted by a certain very senior Maharajah lying up for a marauding leopard which was too quick for him so that he shot off about six inches of the end of its tail. He had the piece mounted and, as a joke, displayed on the wall of the dining room in his summer palace at Mount Abu. Another story concerns a young hopeful who had tethered a goat. After a few nights during which no leopard had appeared he tied a piece of rope round the animal's scrotum, pulling on it from time to time so that its plaintive bleating would advertise its presence, but to no avail. The suspicions of the leopard would no doubt have been aroused by the fact that no goat would be likely to make a noise when situated as precariously as this one was.

Beating for tiger in thick jungle was for the rich. It involved the hiring of a large number of men whose job it was to advance in line towards a point where the priveleged were sitting on elephants waiting for the animals to break cover. There were many cases when a tiger would break back through the line of beaters with fatal consequences to any unwise or unlucky enough to be in its path. There was a pre-first world war story about a wealthy European potentate who, having indulged in a successful day's sport, and having been informed of the mauling of one of the beaters, enquired, on the laying out of the victims of the slaughter, as to the man's fate. On being told that he was dead he said 'then why is he not laid out with the rest?'

Whereas the tiger may, by the general standard of his behaviour, be classed as a gentleman, the leopard is emphatically not. Living principally on barking deer, monkeys, peafowl, and young deer, they will nevertheless kill indiscriminately. Noted for their cunning and ferocity when wounded, they are rightly regarded as vermin to be shot on sight. There was a case of a young officer, recently arrived in India, whose ambition it was to shoot a tiger. All the preliminaries having been carried out he took up a position, as described, up a tree where he spent an unpleasant night being bothered by the myriad of midges and mosquitoes while unable to move in spite of the cold. No tiger appeared to relieve the monotony, and he was relieved to see, at crack of dawn, his hired men arrive to assist him out of the tree.

As the sun rose the jungle burst into life and our hero set out, ahead of the men, along a path which ran along the hillside and which led to the forest bungalow some two miles away where a good breakfast no doubt awaited. Being a novice he failed to take note of the alarm signals indicating the presence of some predator. The loud cries of the peafowl and the general agitation among the bird life; the excited chatter of the colony of langoor monkeys watching from the hilltop trees; and the penetrating barks of the Kakur as it rushes away through the undergrowth. To the experienced shikari these signals would be recognised as a warning, to take care.

Rounding a bend in the path the sportsman froze in his tracks. There, some ten yards ahead of him and facing the same way stood a fine leopard. It was stock still and staring intently into the undergrowth, probably at some small animal which it intended for its breakfast. Its long tail was pointed straight up into the air exposing an intimate target which was irresistible. Forgetting in the excitement that he was carrying only a .22 rifle intended for small game, he took careful aim and fired. Now delivery on that spot of a high velocity bullet with a high killing power: say from a .280 calibre magnum rifle, would either kill the animal outright, or at least paralyse it so as to permit a quick coup de grace in the back of the neck. As it was the small bullet acted as a painful irritant without in any way impeding normal movement by the leopard. It was only after he had fired in the intense excitement of the moment that the officer realised what he had done.

There followed a split second reaction on the part of the wounded animal which, simultaneously with the strike of the bullet, cat-leapt down hill into the thick undergrowth. It was then that the hunter was appalled to hear the sound of woodcutters further down the hill and to realise that he had sent a wounded and enraged leopard in among unarmed men. Without hesitation he cut down into the jungle with the intention of shooting the animal before it could do any damage, only to find that with characteristic cunning it had broken back through the undergrowth and was waiting for him literally with open arms. Seizing his throat in its teeth, it raked him with its cruel and infected claws thus inflicting dreadful injuries from which no man could recover.

Chapter Ten
India: The Great Naturalist

H idden away in the dense forests of the Central Provinces of India there is a clearing with a deep pool of clear spring water which, on a very hot day, can provide welcome relief to the thirsty and to the tired and sweaty.

I was stripping off my clothes prior to plunging in when a quiet cultured voice behind me, slightly tinged with a 'country' accent spoke:

What are you going to do?
Have a swim.
I shouldn't.
Why not?
Snakes: any pool situated in a place like this cannot fail
to house at least one python - and worse.

I replaced my battle dress trousers and climbed back into my jeep next to my passenger whom I was taking to visit a jungle training camp some miles ahead.

The owner of the voice was none other than Jim Corbett, acknowledged as probably the greatest authority on Indian wild life known to modern times. His exploits in tracking down and despatching man-eating tigers and leopards were notorious, often offering himself as a bait in order to attract and outwit these highly dangerous animals, thus relieving large inhabited hill areas of constant threats to their dweller's simple lives. All this out of care for the community in which he lived.

It was indeed a privelege, and an absorbing and enlightening experience to be able to accompany him in the jungle. That this was feasible came about out of the fact that large numbers of British soldiers were arriving in India on their way to fight the Japs in Burma, most of them from an urban background and with an inherent fear of the wild. To overcome this it was decided to institute short courses aimed at promoting interest in the jungle environment and thus creating confidence in the unusual surroundings.

Corbett was the ideal man for the work. He had been born and brought up within reach of the forests where great varieties of wild life had their habitat. Apart from his instinctive understanding of the habits and behaviour of animals large and small he had a natural ability to communicate with great authority and feeling. Armed with Colonel's rank, with deep patriotism, and with an indominatable spirit he readily accepted the task, although it meant long journeys by rail, road or air, under wartime and often extreme climatic conditions, when he was well into his sixties.

On arrival at the various camps he would give lectures, demonstrations and film shows to groups of officers and NCOs who would then 'pass it on'. He would conduct organised strolls through the forest pointing out items of interest such as what can or must not be eaten; used as medicine; or treated as a warning sign of danger; also the animals and snakes to be wary of. At the same time he would look out for unusual events such as to impinge on the imagination of his disciples, and so instill feelings of fascination and familiarity with the environment. He referred to the jungle as his 'detective story' owing to the many clues to be found there, and their solutions.

One such event took place in almost copy book conditions. Accompanied by such a group he stopped under a giant pipul tree. His sharp eyes had caught sight of something unusual in the loose earth under the spreading branches. The hoof marks of a large sambhur stag were plainly imprinted in the dust. Corbett drew the attention of his audience to this, pointing out at the same time that the marks were unusually splayed out. Why? He asked. 'Because something heavy had landed on the animal's back' he replied. What? he asked again. 'Almost certainly a leopard which had been lying along an overhead branch of the pipul tree waiting for such an opportunity' he replied. Then, following the tracks made by the sambhur as its attacker rode it until, at a suitable place, it killed it with a mighty blow from its powerful forearm, its carcass was found hidden under a bush from scavengers. An astonishing piece of detection and deduction.

Returning to our pond in the clearing, as we drove on together he said 'Promise me that you will never go into the jungle alone'. I knew what he meant, but as time went on in the course of my duties I had lapses of memory causing me to take the very risks I had been warned against. There were three such occasions. The first occurred in the course of a reconnaissance of a site for a practice night river crossing. It was a wide river and parallel to and about thirty yards from it there was a 'bund' or embankment some thirty feet high running the whole length of the stream and at about fifty yards from the edge of thick jungle.

Leaving my jeep with my small escort on the main road I walked down the rough cart track which separated the bund from the forest, and therefore cut me off from sound and sight, until I had reached a point about two hundred yards from the road when I climbed up the bund into full view of the river. There I stopped and took stock, but not for long. Coming quite fast towards me from the edge of the stream was what appeared to be a carpet being unrolled. This gathered speed until, on reaching a point about ten yards from where I was standing, it split in two to bypass me on either side. It was then I saw it was snakes, perhaps a hundred or more of all shapes and sizes, disturbed while enjoying their evening drink and anxious to get back to the safety of the jungle, while no doubt prepared to take whatever aggressive action it might prove necessary to do so.

I stood transfixed until the last reptile had wriggled its way past me when, with a gasp of relief, I wasted no time in returning to my escort. The next time I met Jim Corbett I confessed to my folly. His comment: 'So now you know what can happen. Lucky for you there will have been no hamadryad among them, especially a female which usually attacks on sight: fatally.

The next lapse took place shortly after the War in the northern Thai jungles. I was engaged in the training of a Brigade of Dutch ex- POWs not far from the famous Bridge over the River Kwai. I set off one fine morning alone in my jeep to reconnoitre a site for an exercise. As was the rule at that time I was naked from the waist up, so as to take advantage of the allegedly benign properties of the sun. There came a point at which I needed to reverse the vehicle, and in doing so I inadvertently collided with a large clump of bamboo. There came a heavy thud from the back and in the next second I found myself rolling on the ground trying to brush off a number of red ants which were busy biting my bare arms, back and shoulders causing almost unbearable pain.

They were just a few which had become detached from the main nest which had fallen from the clump into the back of the jeep. Had the nest fallen on me it would almost certainly have proved fatal and some days might have passed before I was found: what was left of me.

The third episode occurred at the end of a long night march through thick jungle. A halt was called for a brew up in a veritable pleasance fed by a wide stream sparkling in the warm morning sun. In search of privacy I moved downstream from the main body of our column and, stripping off, sat down comfortably in a rocky side stream forming a natural jacuzzi. While gratefully carrying out my ablutions I saw, out of the corner of my eye, something move. Some ten yards downstream from where I was sitting there was a smooth outcrop of rock flanking the water. From behind this there loomed up what was undoubtedly a King (or Queen) Cobra with hood fully extended. It reared up to a height of about five feet and then stood, in all its fearsome beauty, swaying slightly while inspecting me through what seemed to be rimless pince-nez reminiscent of the headmistress of a 'posh' ladies college. After continuing this scrutiny for some time the reptile obviously decided that I was harmless, as indeed I was from terror, and slowly subsided back behind the rock. For my part I wasted no time in going the other way, still in the 'altogether', while contemplating what might have been my fete had I chosen to go further downstream in the first place, or had the snake been female with young.

Dealing with dangerous animals in the Indian, or any, jungle required a certain professionalism which many sportsmen in their early days had by no means mastered, thus leading to accidents which were seldom trivial. There is a true story of a Himalayan Black Bear which terrorised a group of villages high up in the forest overlooking a wide well-watered valley famous for its lush fruit trees which at certain times of the year attracted these animals. There were three novices camping in this Paradise when they were respectfully approached by a small deputation of woodcutters, inhabitants of the oppressed area. We were their 'mothers and fathers' and this being so would we kindly remove this menace from their midst.

It appeared that more than one of their number had had to run for their lives from unprovoked attacks, and cattle had been destroyed. The Himalayan Black Bear runs up to about six feet in length with a short stumpy tail and a weight of some four hundred pounds. The female is about the same length but two hundred pounds lighter. These animals are or used to be found in large numbers in Kashmir, and from there southwards along the forested hills bordering the Himalayas at a height of about nine thousand feet. They have poor eyesight and hearing but a keen sense of smell. Their diet consists largely of fruit, insects and honey, but older bears tend to eat flesh, notably sheep and cattle, often killing large numbers.

According to our deputation the bear's feeding ground lay at some five thousand feet above where we were encamped, approachable by a single steep rough track which ran along the side of the mountain. The plan was to leave at mid-night thus allowing for arrival on the ground at first light, and then to play it from there. Shortly after the time of departure, however, a thunder storm of great ferocity broke over our heads turning the whole countryside into a vast waterfall, with all the streams becoming fast and noisy torrents, and the forest slopes into mud slides.

Slow progress was made, however, until, as dawn was breaking, the villagers signalled that we were on the feeding ground where the bear had been seen on several days running. A thin drizzle was still falling and the visibility was poor but improving. Of the two officers involved one was carrying a 375 Magnum rifle, a clumsy weapon in these conditions but the only heavy rifle available; the other had a Winchester Repeater 300, far too light for dealing with a dangerous animal of any size. The urgent need to dispose of the bear before it could do any more harm seemed to excuse the palpable shortage of suitable equipment for the task in hand.

As the small party stood hesitantly on the track looking down the hillside, almost by appointment a bear appeared in the long grass some thirty yards below plodding its way in the opposite direction and parallel to the pathway along which they had come. This came as a surprise, but an even greater one was that following in echelon behind the animal were two half grown cubs. The bear was a female and, having young, infinitely 'more deadly than the male'. A whispered consultation then took place and it was decided that the officer with the Winchester, accompanied by the shikari, or guide, who had attached himself to the party, would make his way back along the path with the intention of making a noise and thereby turning the animal's back across the grassy clearing and thus offering a fair target to the officer with the Magnum who would by then have taken up a commanding position above the path giving a field of view.

All seemed set when, from a point where there was a sharp bend in the path, there came the sound of a shot. It subsequently transpired that the bear, perhaps becoming suspicious, had turned uphill, breaking cover only a few yards from the officer with the Winchester and continuing its climb followed by the cubs while taking no notice of its intending destroyer. The latter, hopelessly nonplussed at the way things were moving, yielded to exhortations by the shikari to shoot and did so at the animal's broad backside about ten yards above him.

The calibre of bullet was such as to cause acute pain, but little else except to infuriate the animal as well as provoke its maternal instincts. It rounded and charged angrily down the hill seeking to wreak vengeance on whoever had inflicted the injury. The first that the officer with the magnum knew of this was when the shikari appeared around the bend running as fast as his spindly legs would carry him on the slippery path, his face distorted with terror, until executing a graceful swallow dive into some rhododendron bushes further down the slope. Next came the erstwile marksman. Turning bravely to face his pursuer, he found himself knocked into a sitting position on the path while suffering a severe mauling until man and animal rolled over together down the steep hillside.

The witnesses to all this had been some distance away. When they reached the point on the path where the two had disappeared they found thick undergrowth lining the slope and no sign of the officer. However one of the party caught sight of the hindquarters of the bear as it made off in a hurry further down the hillside. A frantic search revealed the officer in a semi-conscious state lying against a sapling, and bleeding profusely from deep bite wounds to the arms and legs, but fortunately spared the awful disfigurement of the face so often inflicted by these animals with their steel-shod claws.

There followed an anxious period during which the wounded man was carried, part way on a litter and part way by piggy back, to a German mission hospital some seven miles down the valley. The German doctor, after carrying out a thorough inspection, relieved everyone's feelings by stating: 'So the bear he bit, but no doubt he is not cleaning his teeth first'. Within a week or two all was well with the patient. As to the bear an organised follow up indicated that after no doubt licking her wounds, she and her cubs had moved to pastures new.

PART 3:
UGANDA/KENYA
1955-1965

Patrick Hearn landed in Uganda in January 1955, with Cynthia and the four children arriving on the S.S. Kenya Castle London-Mombasa on 27 April. He sent a cable on his arrival: "Arrived safely, first expectations excellent!" and note now that his infectious optimism is a characteristic of our family.

Uganda in the late 1950's was exciting. Pat plunged into his responsibilities, one of which was the development of the parks and wildlife service. A safari was arranged around the amazing wildlife reserves in western Uganda, under the Ruwenzori "Mountains of the Moon". Family drives at weekends were enjoyed to the Queen Elisabeth dam at Jinja, one of the sources of the Nile, and to Entebbe on Lake Victoria (in July 1976 the site of the heroic "Entebbe Raid" by the Israelis to release their hostages).

After two years, Patrick Hearn was informed by the British government that his contract was up soon and he should return with the family to UK and await renewal - if there was no Ugandan who could do the job. Having moved the family to Uganda and settled well, with the older children at excellent boarding schools in Nairobi, Pat completed his contract and joined a busy legal practice in Nairobi. He then alternated a couple of years each in Nairobi and in Jinja Uganda as events drove opportunities.

Meanwhile the geopolitics were also alternating, with independence developments throughout Africa. Pat was in favour of accelerated training and independence for Africans in a transition, and he also appeared often pro-bono as a barrister for African clients who he felt had been wronged in the legal system. He worked also with Madhvani Sugar in Jinja, a hugely hard working and successful Indian family and enterprise.

By the late 1950's, the clouds were gathering. On the positive side the Mau Mau rebellion in Kenya was coming to an end. The British government announced that Uganda and Kenya would gain independence by the early sixties, but excluded the settlers and expatriates in Kenya from participation in discussions of freedom "Uhuru".

Kenya could potentially have set a standard for Africa in integrating the "white tribe" into independence, working for a truly multidisciplinary nation. Kenyatta implied this in his slogan "Harambee" – pull together, teamwork. But neither Whitehall nor Nairobi worked much on that option and the opportunity was lost in the flow of history as the British rapidly ceded control.

By the early 1960's, Pat Hearn was a successful lawyer in Nairobi. The shadows were gathering with the waves of corruption and violence. Kenyatta and his wife Mama Ngina were taking an increasing share. Patrick was increasingly concerned about the quality of education for his younger three children. The tipping point came when he was phoned by a Minister and informed that his legal practice was to be half-owned by the Minister's brother, who had no legal experience. Pat was never slow to make decisions, about individuals or about situations. The family arrived on England's green and pleasant land in early 1966.

This completes the wider international career of Patrick Hearn, the subjects of his writings, and of this book. He continued full steam, working for the Treasury Solicitors in London, winning the key case on retail price maintenance; and then as legal counsel to Reed Paper corporation, working on mergers and acquisitions across Europe. He found his age-required retirement at the age of 65 in 1977 an unwelcome challenge, but settled to his fourth career – soldier, lawyer, businessman, writer. He published four well received books on "The Law for International Business"; a revision of his father's book "The Seven Cities of Delhi" (1906) reprinted in India in 2006; and then this book: "The Vintage Year 1912". Patrick Hearn, then aged 90, gave his son John the manuscript of this book in Canberra in 2002 and asked him to aim at publication.

Patrick Hearn continued to make waves until his death in Eastbourne on 20th January 2004.

"Do not go easy into that goodnight. Fight, fight against the dying of the light…" (Dylan Thomas)

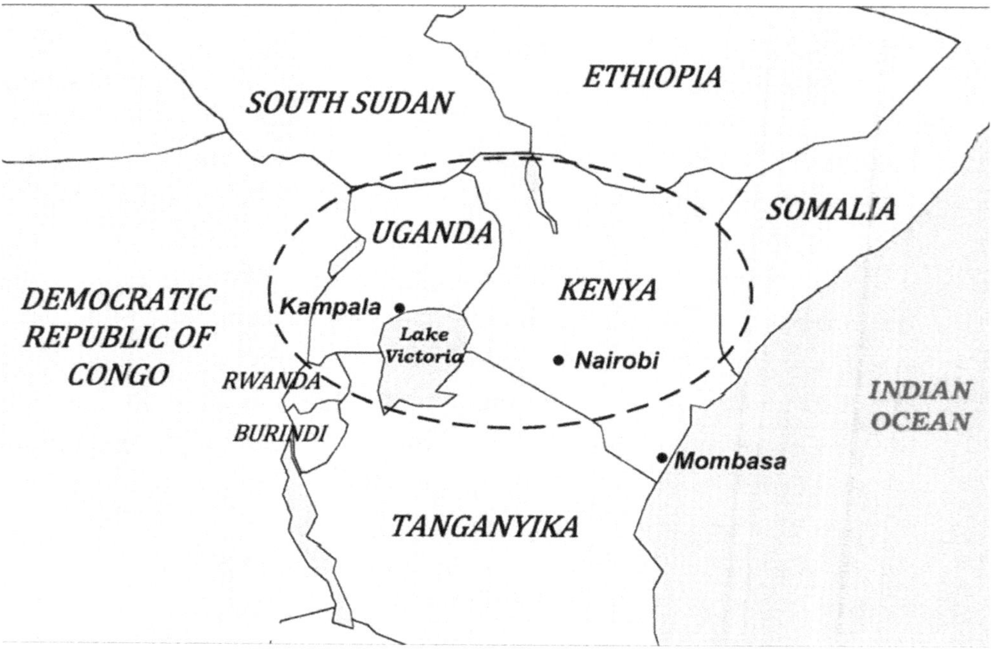

Figure 12: 1950s East Africa; Uganda and Kenya

Figure 13: Barrister and Corporate Legal Adviser, London 1954

Figure 14: *Arrived in Uganda - 1955*

Back row: Simon, Susan, John
Front row: Mary, Cynthia, Paul, Patrick

Figure 15: *Legal Practice, Jinja Uganda 1962*

Figure 16: Oxford, 80th Birthday 1992

Figure 17: The Law for Business - 1987 and 1992

Figure 18: The Law for Business - 1979 and 1981

Chapter Eleven
Uganda: Pearl of Africa

His name was Willy. He was wearing a gunner tie, an I Zingari blazer, and a broad smile which showed up the fine healthy polish of his ebony face. He announced himself as anxious to become my slave for life, and to that end he produced a bundle of 'baruas': references which must have belonged to his grandfather, or somebody else's! They did not always say quite the right thing. Nevertheless the smile was irresistible, and we entered into a partnership contract which in due course was to survive the arrival of the memsahib and to endure for many years, in spite of a few accidents.

Willy was my introduction to East Africa. He entered on his duties with startling enthusiasm, filling the bath with boiling water and therein washing my brand new white sharkskin dinner jacket, my dressing gown, and my bedroom slippers! In the future, whenever one of the family turned up wearing something particularly scruffy, the cry went up 'Willy washed it'. But he learnt. Another acquisition was Jessica, a handsome, upstanding (in more ways than one) Toro girl with many admirers which did not prevent her from serving us faithfully and with great dignity and patience for many years, as lady's maid, governess, and general female factotum.

Uganda, which was where we were for the time being, was for many in those piping days of the mid nineteen fifties a choice place to be. Not being a colony, but a protectorate ruled under treaty, there were no white settlers to provide a target for dissent. At the same time, by African standards, the country and its people were rich. The principal primary products were cotton and coffee. The cotton was long staple up to Egyptian quality and thus commanding high prices in world markets; the coffee being mainly Robusta with a high acid content, particularly popular in Germany and also much used in the blending of 'instant' brands. These products were sold abroad through marketing boards which paid a fixed and not ungenerous price to the African producer, while earning a good profit for the Treasury for expenditure on roads, railways, schools and hospitals, all to a high standard.

Tea was also at this time beginning to be produced, the soil being particularly suited to its growth. Tobacco was grown in considerable quantities in the north feeding a thriving cigarette industry based on Jinja, in eastern Uganda, and in Nairobi.

Another important product was sugar, cultivated and refined at two fine large estates near Jinja, on Lake Victoria. These were in the hands of wealthy, hard working and public spirited Indian families. The founder of one of the family companies had arrived in East Africa from Kathiawar in Western India in the first few years of this century to work as a low paid clerk on the railway, then under construction. A man of great energy and vision he had early on recognised the future which existed for sugar production in Uganda. It was not an easy thing, in those prejudiced days, to persuade the ruling power to accede to requests for land use made by 'greedy' Asians, the paramount policy being quite properly the protection and advancement of the rights and welfare of the indigenous people.

But he achieved a limited success in the first instance, obtaining a lease of a thousand acres. This, after many years of perseverance and endeavour, was transformed into a plantation of some twenty five thousand acres employing, together with other pioneering industries, some thirteen thousand Africans. This was a triumph for private enterprise needing courage and skill of a very high order. The benefits in the form of industrial expansion became spread out all over East Africa. Over a relatively short period of time there rose up factories for the manufacture of cotton textiles, glassware, metal boxes, beer, constructional steel, and other such substantial enterprises.

Uganda is a land of striking scenic versatility. Great lakes, high mountains, fast rivers and, particularly in the centre and south, lush vegetation, all to be savoured in a relatively short space of time, combined with a huge variety of animal and bird life to create a veritable paradise for the visitor. Crossing the border from Kenya, and ignoring for the time being the macadamised road leading to the fleshpots of Kampala, the traveller might turn right passing, on the way to the bustling town of Mbale, the five hundred foot high Tororo Rock, home of many noisy baboons. Near to the base of this rock there was a hotel which, between the wars, was owned and meticulously managed by a retired Scottish sea captain. The rooms were spotless, the food wholesome and well cooked, and the African staff immaculately turned out, efficient, and clearly happy and contented.

Mine host tended to be cantankerous at times, especially when the strict but not unreasonable rules which he considered it necessary to impose were in any way transgressed. He liked to run his establishment as he had no doubt run his ship - as he wished. Over the entrance to the hotel appeared the ominous words: 'Hamish MacTavish, or something equally Caledonian. Licensed to sell what he likes, when he pleases, to whom he chooses, at whatever price he cares to charge'. He was known to turn away visitors of whom, for one reason or another, he disapproved. Thus a party of a certain nationality which he disliked were denied hospitality and had to go a long way to the next hostelry. On another occasion no less a dignitary than the Governor incurred his wrath when his driver, ignoring the signposts indicating the car park, drove up in a cloud of dust to the front entrance only to be told curtly to go back, without getting out of the car.

At Mbale, some twenty eight miles from Tororo, and at the foot of Mount Elgon which offers a stiff three day climb to nearly fifteen thousand feet for those so minded, the road forks. To the right it runs due north to the wilderness of Karamoja, thick with game and peopled largely by tall handsome tribesmen, usually naked and carrying spears as well as, reputedly, the longest John Thomases in Africa which is saying a lot. In support of this claim photographs have been witnessed in one of which a gentleman had literally tied himself in a knot. This brings to mind a wartime story about Winston Churchill.

It appears that in preparation for the D Day landings some large rubber containers, about three feet long by one foot in circumference, designed for floating ashore small items of military stores, had been found wanting under test. Hundreds of thousands of these had therefore become surplus, and nobody could think what to do with them. As, seemingly, with everything else, Churchill was asked. After staring at one of them quizzically for a minute he removed his cigar: "Send them to Russia..emm.. and label them 'Made in England..emm..medium size'!

Taking the left hand fork a long and somewhat dusty drive through flat and featureless country brings us to what must be one of the showpieces of Africa. This is the Murchison Falls Game Park (now renamed Kabalega Falls National Park). This consists of some fifteen hundred square miles of bush cut down the middle by the river Nile on its way north from Lake Victoria at Ripon Falls, first discovered by Speke in 1862. At the head of Murchison Falls there is a twenty foot gap through which a huge volume of water plunges some one hundred and thirty feet to resume its onward journey. Legend has it that once a young brave, in search of his girl, took a running jump over this gap. Some girl!

Seven miles downstream from this point there was a comfortable game lodge where it was an outstanding experience to be able to sit over a drink in the evening and watch, in the rosy hue thrown by the setting sun, great herds of elephant and other game as they came down to the river to drink or bathe. From the lodge it was possible to proceed by motor launch up river to near the foot of the Falls, and from there, under escort, to follow a path to the top. The whole area abounds with game of every description. Elephant, lion, rhino, cheetah, buffalo, also many different varieties of monkey, gazelle, and antelope including the Uganda Kob and the Impala. In the water and along the river banks may be seen large numbers of hippopotamus and of crocodile, the latter lining the banks, some with their hideous mouths wide open to enable the scavenging egrets, their self appointed dental hygenists, to pick their teeth free of masticated fish and other debris.

There was a story in those days of a young visitor with a touring party proceeding by launch up the middle of the river. After a bit he stripped off to reveal a fine sun-tanned Tarzanian torso. In full view of the pretty girls on the launch, and the not so pretty crocodiles on the banks, he dived into the water to follow the launch with an effortless crawl until, after a hundred yards or so he clambered aboard to the loud applause of the company. Asked if he had not stretched his luck a bit he replied, sotto voce, that there was no danger because crocodiles did not venture into deep water and he knew that the centre of the river was all of this.

The following day the party again chartered the launch, this time deciding to troll for nile perch with the use of a powerful rod and line fixed to the rear of the boat. The lure was got up to resemble a tiger fish, a favoured item in the perch's diet. A fish eagle, from its look out at the top of a tree, spotted this, and taking it for the real thing, swooped down, picked it up in its talons and, becoming entangled with the hooks, fell on the water. Almost immediately, with a frightening swirl and a crash, a crocodile struck. Away went eagle, lure, rod, line and all, never to be seen again. The launch was in midstream. Tarzan, who had been about to repeat his performance, turned ashen.

One of the outstanding attractions of Uganda is the variety of bird life and its accessibility. In the well wooded country along the length of the Victoria Nile birds of many hundreds of colourful feathers may be freely witnessed and photographed. Some experts have held it to be the best place in Africa for this purpose. By the river below Murchison can be seen, among other species, rare breeds of duck, also herons, storks, and birds of prey, while in the more wooded areas may be found such African exotica as the small Yellow-Breasted Sunbird, the bright yellow plumage offset by its green head and prominent blue throat; the sober long-tailed Widow Bird, black with long twenty four inch tail; the Gorgeous Bush Shrike, resplendent though murderous in vivid yellow and green, with red throat and prominent blue-black collar; and the exquisitely coloured Emerald Cuckoo. Indeed everywhere one went there was a good chance of spotting one or other of the various species of flycatcher, including the famed birds of paradise; pied kingfishers; golden orioles, and crested barbets.

The rich harvest of experience to be gleaned from the Park required that not less than a week's stay could do it full justice. During such a period of time it was possible to make daily excursions to vantage points where patience would sooner or later be rewarded by some interesting or spectacular sight, a pride of lions hunting down and killing their prey for example. But many would agree that by far the most engaging, interesting, and unpredictable animal in East Africa was and, in sadly reduced numbers it would seem, must remain the elephant. The media have ensured that by now everyone must be well aware of what they eat, where they live, and how they make love. But they also possess an individuality which distinguishes them from most other denizens of the wild, and from each other, and which can only be appreciated by means of observation over a fair period of time.

A recent estimate indicates that Murchison may hold up to fourteen thousand elephant, in spite of reports of serious inroads by poachers over a good many years. Anyone motoring through the Park might expect to encounter a herd crossing the track. These large beasts have a remarkable ability to move silently and unobtrusively so that before you are aware of their presence you may find yourself surrounded. In such an event the only answer is to stop, look, and wait, sometimes for an hour or more if they are in a loitering mood. There was once a learned judge, a keen fisherman, who liked to tell the story, which he did very well, of how one evening he was fishing for trout in a delightful stream called the Rupengazi. This bustling river runs down the eastern flank of Mount Kenya past where there used to be, and perhaps there still is, a pleasant hotel suitably named the Isaac Walton. Both banks of the stream are fairly thickly wooded so that any fly caster must wade, and this our judge was doing when he heard a slight noise behind him. Looking round he saw, only a few yards behind, the head and tusks of a huge pachiderm. He confessed: 'Only my laundryman came to know how frightened I was'.

Returning to Murchison there was, at the time we are talking about, an old tusker who came to be known as the Lord Mayor. He had settled down, quite uninvited, to pass his declining years at the Lodge which he used to patrol regularly at night and sometimes by day. Visitors were warned to give him a wide berth, and the Parks staff remained uneasily watchful. One day he prevented an alarmed Governor who was visiting the place from leaving his launch by simply standing on the landing stage, flapping his ears, and raising his trunk. On another occasion he came across a car containing two sleeping German tourists. The windows were open and there was an irresistible bunch of bananas in the back seat. Groping around with his trunk in search of this delicacy he woke one of the men who, not knowing in the dark what sort of intruder it was, lashed out. In a second the elephant had flipped the car over onto its roof. As time went on he became increasingly possessive, touchy and unpredictable until for the general safety he had to be professionally destroyed. Surrounded by such a herd as has been described the motorist would be afforded a unique opportunity of studying the animals in their natural habitat. He would find them to be very family conscious beasts, often behaving almost like humans in their dealings with each other. On one such occasion there took place an amusing incident. A family group of elephants were standing under a tree, among them seemingly the pretty daughter who was being shamelessly ogled by what was obviously a 'handlebar Harry' type of roué. Mother contented herself with looking on disapprovingly, but Father was not having any. He seemed to stroll up meaningfully to tell the interloper to hop it, which he did with alacrity.

But such game watching was not without its perils. A parks warden similarly caught left the engine of his car running so as to seize any sudden opportunity of escape which might present itself. One of the small elephants, inquisitive like all children, grasped the exhaust pipe in its trunk. There was a squeal of pain and Mum not only turned the car over but put her foot on it as well. Fortunately the warden got away with only a nasty shock.

What comes as a surprise to many is how it is that elephants and other occupants of the Parks and Reserves seem to know with uncanny accuracy the extent of the area in which they can expect protection from the hunter's bullet, and the poacher's trap. It was said that at a time of the year when the sorgum seeds were ripe on the bushes, parties of elephant would leave the reserve by night to feed off these delicacies. One mighty intake of nature's vacuum cleaner could completely strip a plant, which was bad luck on the farmer. The real fun started, however, when fermentation took place in the animals' stomachs. Word was that they could be seen rollicking home at crack of dawn in a drunken condition, leaning against each other for mutual support while having a gay old time. Perhaps they were trumpetting out the boozer's version of 'The Soldier's Chorus' from Gounod's Faust.

Mention of nile perch is a reminder of one of Uganda's unusual sporting attractions. Lake Albert, which divides Uganda from Zaire and in which the Victoria Nile merges with the Albert Nile to continue to flow northwards through the Sudan and Egypt to the Mediterranean, houses many of these fish which grow up to a considerable size, often well over one hundred pounds in weight. As has been partly explained they may best be caught by the process of trolling. That is to say drawing a lure through the water at a distance of about thirty yards behind a launch by means of a strong line attached to a powerful rod operated by an automatic reel. When the perch takes the lure the act of doing so propels it high into the air so that those in the launch know that they have 'got something on'. The fish then sounds - goes to the bottom, taking with it a great deal of line heavily weighted by the action of the automatic reel which needs to be wound in as soon as the line slackens, which means that the perch is again on its way to and through the surface to execute another spectacular leap, this time much nearer the launch, while trying desperately to divest itself of the hooks. There then follows a steady pull-in with the odds heavily against the fish until, on sighting the bottom of the boat, it makes a last desperate leap to about seven feet before collapsing on the water and coming tamely to the gaff. All very spectacular but 'ce n'est pas la guerre'.

Altogether this is tame sport when compared with big-game fishing for marlin, sailfish, barracuda, shark and kingfish which can be indulged in off Mombasa or Malindi on the Kenya coast.

But it makes for a good and interesting day out, and the real pleasure comes from eating what is acknowledged to be a gourmet's delight. There was a story going the rounds in Cairo during the war about the German commander, Field Marshal Rommel. It appears that, in 1942, after he had chased the British Eighth Army all the way down the Desert Road until, coming to a halt some fifty miles from Alexandria, he was poised to advance on Cairo, which he was confident of capturing. He sent a signal to Goering inviting him and his Fuehrer to dine with him on a given date at the Mena House Hotel, near the Pyramids, the principal item on the Menu to be nile perch. As we know the engagement had to be postponed indefinitely.

There is no doubt that these big fish, cut up and properly cooked, make superb eating. With a well defined and easily removed backbone, and with any other bones similarly disposable, the firm flesh can be cut into convenient steaks. The best and simplest method of cooking is by baking. Place the fish in a medium oven in a baking dish with plenty of butter, some chopped onion and parsley, a little basil and some salt and pepper. Half an hour later, or when it is nearly cooked, pour over it a glass of a good dry white wine, perhaps a Pouilly Fuisse or a Chablis. Give it another five minutes, then tuck in to the accompaniment of the rest of the bottle of wine.

Chapter Twelve
Uganda: The Hill of the Antelope

Proceeding on our tour of Uganda, after sampling what Lake Albert has to offer, we should go southwards, first to the kingdom of Toro to find Fort Portal, a prosperous township nestling at the foot of Mt Ruwenzori, allegedly Haggard's 'Mountains of the Moon', steeped in legend and superstition, and rising to over sixteen thousand feet. Then on past railhead at Kasese and the Ruwenzori National Park; round, or if you wish through, the Impenetrable Forest to Kabale: Uganda's highest town at over six thousand feet and the centre of many attractions, causing the area to be called the 'Switzerland of Africa'. Some twenty five miles to the west of the town is the Kanaba gap overlooking the volcanoes on the borders of Zaire and Rwanda Urundi, Mounts Muhavura and Gahinga, thirteen thousand and eleven thousand feet in height respectively, home of the mountain gorillas. The view from here is considered by many to be one of the finest in the whole of Africa.

As with Murchison the area has many natural amenities worthy of relaxed exploration and a reasonably long stop-over. Returning eastwards from there one passes through the old kingdom of Ankole with its famous long horned cattle, and its capital at Mbarara at three thousand six hundred feet. Another one hundred miles or so on we come to Masaka, in the centre of a rich coffee growing area. A road to the right leads south to the Tanzania border at the Kagera River, while we must proceed northwards a distance of eighty miles to Kampala, crossing the Equator after thirty miles.

Thirty years ago Kampala - the hill of the antelope - was a most pleasant garden city. Built on and among a number of green hills, several of them crowned by places of religious worship, it was a mixture of modern government and institutional buildings; hotels and offices; sprawling Asian shops; and, on the periphery, banana groves concealing many African houses, mainly rondavels, and villages. Close to the centre, concentrated on higher ground, there were low density bungaloid residences occupied by Europeans, mostly civil servants; senior business men preferring to live in more distinctive houses in more open surroundings. Asians, except for the more wealthy, lived mostly over or behind their shops or business premises in the low lying city centre. There was a thriving European social club, and an excellent golf club down in the valley.

As throughout the British colonial empire there was little social integration between the races. There was also not much violent crime except as between Africans, and that usually when under the influence of drugs or drink. The latter was a problem. To go for a pleasant drive around Kampala in the cool of a Sunday evening was to be witness to many comic scenes of drunkenness. Robust Buganda ladies, colourfully dressed in their voluminous and gaily printed garments known as 'busutis' a form of national dress, could be seen apparently unconcerned with their senseless husbands slung across their shoulders, or draped in a state of ignominious collapse over the cross bars of bicycles, being removed to where they could sleep off what was obviously the most appalling binge. 'Pombe' was the main culprit, a lethal brew fermented from sorghum or millet, particularly effective and lethal when sucked through a straw.

As has been indicated, a feature of the Kampala landscape was the merging of buildings into a lush green environment with plenty of open space. In achieving this, efficient town planning in early days had had the assistance of nature. On one of the hills overlooking the city there was an elegantly constructed and beautifully sited house which was the residence of a European VIP and his wife. Terraced lawns edged with rose beds led down into a valley along which ran a quietly babbling brook. On these terraces there strolled a small colony of crested cranes to create a scene of dignified enchantment. But even paradise has its blemishes. In this case it took the ungainly shape of a geriatric male parrot, the lady's pride and joy. Mean and cantankerous, he would emerge from his living quarters deep in the recesses of the house at an hour when the sun had had time to warm up the tiles on the verandah. Here he would squat and scratch himself prior to descending on to the lawn for his morning constitutional. Staring round malevolently he would scream abuse at any African servant who, in the course of his household duties, had the temerity to disturb his privacy.

One day the old creature was doing his walkabout on the lawn when out of the sky there swooped a large kite. Seizing the many coloured object in its talons it took off for the bush. There was a shocked silence. Then the air was rent by shouts of enraged invective, turning to cries of alarm as the ground began to recede. But the wily old bird knew a thing or two. In a high falsetto, emulating the authoritative voice of his mistress, he shouted out: 'lete chae lete chae' (bring tea). This was enough to bring the servants running from behind the house whereupon the predator, no doubt thinking it had picked up more than it had bargained for, dropped its noisy load.

Its descent broken by a rose bush, the infuriated parrot ran for the protective cover of the verandah, swearing blue murder as he went. It was at least a week before he again ventured out. He spent much of it with his head tucked under his wing, peering out from time to time to utter foul curses. When he did resume his normal habits it was noticed that, before stepping down on the grass, he spent a good deal of time scanning the sky for intruders.

Twenty one miles due south of Kampala is what was the seat of the protectorate government: Entebbe. Here, at three thousand seven hundred feet above sea level, were situated Government House, the administrative offices, and the houses of the posher civil servants: the 'administration'. There was the usual club, a good hotel, and the international airport, scene many years later of the daring and brilliantly executed Israeli rescue operation. The Uganda Civil Service was organised on a three tier system as in all British colonial territories. The top layer was 'the administration' consisting mainly of arts graduates from Oxbridge. Some of the post war intake gave the impression of regarding themselves as being a considerable cut above the common stream; of apeing the intellectual; and giving far too much attention to protocol and as to who sat where at dinner parties. But there may sometimes have been skeletons among the files in their official cupboards.

There was a sorry tale told of long ago when a new judge arrived on appointment to the Uganda High Court. He brought with him a reputation for a certain independence of character. After a decent interval to satisfy protocol, he and his wife were invited to dine with the Chief Secretary. Among the few others asked was the Attorney General. In view of the judge's reputation it came as no surprise that they arrived half an hour late; but it came as something of a shock, in view of the exalted position of the host, when it became apparent that they had both had a lot more than their fair share of the hard stuff. The company had hardly sat down to dinner when the judge's wife keeled over and her head fell in the soup. Her hostess, a kind and gracious lady, expressed her concern: 'I am so sorry you are not feeling well, my dear', and started to wring the stuff out of her hair, only to be told by the judge, in the crudest terms, to 'leave off'. At this the Attorney General, hoping to be of assistance, hurried round the table only to be felled by a mighty blow. The host, a tall and distinguished gentleman, then approached to be met by: 'Not another step - or I'll knock your block off'. The evening broke up in disorder and it hardly needs to be added that after that the judge's tenure of office was shortlived.

These administrative civil servants were engaged either in the field as district officers doing whatever they do; or in the secretariat at Entebbe, sitting on their bottoms and dealing with the bumph. But it has to be said that Uganda was a well run and happy country in those days. The second layer was the executive branch: a wide conglomeration of so called specialist experts, nearly all European, few of them graduates. This took in trade officers, cooperative officers, labour officers, meat inspectors, drain inspectors, community development officers, and many others who did God knew what. An outspoken lady, wife of a senior company director, when asked at a dinner party the identity of a man sitting further down the table, replied with a sniff: 'Drains, I expect'. This seemed to sum it up.

The large number and variety of these officers and inspectors gave rise to quite a lot of unfavourable comment on the part of those who had to foot the bill. Few were vested with any real skills which could not have been developed locally; all had the right to home leave for three months in every eighteen; and they were able to live to a much inflated standard of living. This was the system, and those benefitting from it could hardly be blamed for doing so. In any case they did a good enough job within its limits. But East African settlers and business men could also hardly be blamed for asking: why so many? and why a fair proportion at least of the jobs could not be given to the many reasonably educated Africans who could have done with them? These might well have profitted from the experience of working under the pupillage of trained British administrators. As it was, when independence loomed up suddenly wide gaps were left to be filled by untrained Africans who in the event tried hard and did well enough.

But serious difficulties inevitably arose which should have been foreseen. In an attempt to correct these, 'crash courses' were introduced in some areas of activity. One such was aimed at training Africans to replace European and Indian train drivers. Some wit wrote to the papers accounting the scheme a marked success, reporting that there had been seventy four crashes on the railway in the first six months. But they quickly improved.

The third tier of colonial government was the clerical branch. This was manned by Africans and Asians whose role was relatively menial. Standing separate from the administrative branches were the professionals. These included judges and other members of the colonial legal service; medicos; vets; architects; agriculturists; educationists; police and many other categories who played a direct part in the development of the territories. Also included were those who ran the postal service; the railways; the docks and harbours; roads; and other essential quasi-government infrastructural institutions. All of these were well qualified and experienced men who made a valuable, indeed indispensable, contribution to the territories, and East Africa was well served by them.

Some insight into the way of life of the rural African could be gained in the course of proceedings in the courts of law. It is probably accurate to say that in all British colonial possessions the law was based on English common law as modified by local legislation according to Territorial needs. Criminal law was set out in the Penal Code applicable to the territory, and any specific statutory provisions, the offences being a lot less numerous and much more easy of definition than was the case in more sophisticated countries. Unlawful killing was seldom premeditated and often resulted from sudden quarrels originating in an excess of drink or drugs. Murder was punishable by hanging. Grievous bodily harm or rape could be rewarded by up to twenty four strokes of the cane, a severe punishment which was greatly feared.

Two cases of alleged murder come to mind as being of special human interest. The first concerned a Lake Victoria fisherman. He owned his own boat on the lake and was therefore a prosperous man by local standards. He also proved to be a popular figure among his peers, and he was married to a very pretty wife who was the indirect cause of his being charged with the murder by stabbing of a man not far from his home. The prosecution case was that the dead man had been having, or seeking to have, an affair with the accused's wife. One night, thinking that the husband was away fishing, he was said to have visited the house, only to find him very much in residence so that he had to run for it. Caught up with he was killed by stab wounds deep in the lumbar region.

The pre-trial depositions were such as to indicate a long and more than usually complicated case. There were many witnesses and much conflicting evidence. This being so the trial judge decided, under a form of legal aid scheme then in force, to employ a European advocate from Nairobi to conduct the defence. The trial took place in Jinja, near to the source of the Victoria Nile, where the courthouse stood on its own in the middle of a large grassy compound. The accused pleaded not guilty. His story was that at the time the deed was said to have taken place he was on his boat with two chums who testified accordingly. Although he was acquainted with the dead man he had no relationship with him, nor had he any knowledge of any visit he may have made to his house, nor had his wife. The prosecution produced witnesses to say that the two friends, instead of being on the accused's boat were, in fact, drinking together in a bar at the time. However under cross examination this evidence turned out to be highly suspect.

The prosecution also produced what they said was a fisherman's knife with a curiously shaped blade and distinctive marks on the handle which had been found near the body and which they said belonged to the accused. This he strenuously denied, saying that he had never seen it before. But they were quite unable to corroborate the story that the dead man had visited the accused's house, or had any relationship with his wife. What they did do however was to exhibit a pair of trousers which had been taken from the house. There was forensic evidence that these had recently been washed but that traces of blood had been detected on the trouser legs. This was a nasty one for the defence. However cross examination revealed that the blood was all on the back of the legs and in very small spots only, there was no general staining.

These facts created a flaw in the prosecution case which counsel was able to exploit. First it was not seen how a man could stab another in the body and get only very small bloodstains, and those on the back of the trousers low down, there being none at all in the front. Second, spots of blood could very well be present in an insect ridden country like Uganda, resulting from a person scratching 'dudu' bites. Many witnesses were called on either side, and the case lasted for three weeks, ending in acquittal.

Throughout the whole of the trial a vast throng of spectators, mostly women in gay apparel, had stood or sat silently both in the courtroom and outside in the compound. When the verdict was announced and the judge told the accused that he was free to go they rose to their feet amid loud cries of delight accompanied by noisy ululation. The latter is a pulsating and extremely penetrating sound made by women tapping their mouths while uttering a high pitched single note call. They say that such a sound will be taken up and repeated all the way down the dark continent until finally subsiding at the Cape. Who knows? In the meanwhile the erstwhile prisoner, finding an open window conveniently placed next to the dock where he had stood for so long, jumped out and took to his heels across the compound, no doubt to make his escape before the judge and the three African assessors could change their minds. He was hotly pursued all the way home by a phalanx of cheering, singing and dancing ladies, and the pombe will assuredly have flown generously for several days thereafter.

Back in Nairobi the relieved counsel for the defence, discussing the case with his partner, expressed the opinion that although he had had to put a great deal of sustained effort into the trial which had remained finely balanced to the end, he would nevertheless never see the man again, there being no gratitude among such people. He was wrong. A few weeks later he was in his chambers when a visitor was announced. It was Simon the fisherman. With him he had his attractive young wife and two quite adorable children, beautifully dressed little girls each carrying posies which they presented with carefully rehearsed curtsies. They had travelled four hundred miles for the purpose. It made it all doubly worthwhile.

The other case had a sadder ending. An African farmer, who owned a relatively substantial cotton plantation in the Busoga district of Uganda where the soil is well suited to that purpose, had killed his wife. He was put on trial for murder, and the same counsel was sent for from Nairobi for the same reason. The story was that he loved his wife by whom he had had ten healthy children. Sadly, so late in their lives together, she had fallen prey to an interloper with whom she had taken up residence some miles away. Now, under African customary law, as distinct from the English system, adultery is a crime punishable by imprisonment.

Much to the man's regret, and more in order to break up the romance than through any wish to see her punished, he had her brought before the elders and she was sentenced to a year in jail. Came Ugandan independence day and in the midst of the general rejoicing an amnesty was declared. On the day when she was to be released he waited expectantly at the bus stop, but when a good deal of time had gone by and she did not appear he drew his own sad conclusion and went with a heavy heart to seek her at the home of his rival. She was there. Rushing out at the sight of him she uncharacteristically and no doubt from guilt heaped volleys of abuse and insult on him and, what was worse, his manhood. Distressed and utterly confused he lashed out at her with his knife, which all African farmers habitually carry on their persons. Unfortunately he struck her in the stomach, killing her.

Counsel thought long and hard about this. He was much taken by his client's demeanour. Tall and humbly dignified, he was utterly truthful, and obviously appalled at what he had done. His action had been impulsive and retaliatory, at no time can he have wished it to have a fatal result. But how to convince the judge and the assessors that this was so and thus reduce the charge. Acquittal was clearly out of the question so that a plea of not guilty of murder but guilty of manslaughter was entered. The prosecution wanted none of it. English law, which prevailed, was clear. Mere abuse, however insulting did not constitute provocation sufficient to reduce a charge of murder to one of manslaughter, and a person must be taken to intend the natural consequence of his act.

Counsel was thrown back on an attempt to argue this from an African point of view, on the basis that in the social environment peculiar to the African certain circumstances created differences of emphasis and therefore impact and that this should be taken into account in assessing culpability. A seemingly strong point was made that owing to the fact that adultery was a crime under customary law, its discovery by the husband must be accorded a greater degree of provocation than would be the case in England. All this was to no avail and the accused was found guilty and sentenced to death. In his final address to the court counsel repeated these argument with an eye to a rule, peculiar to colonial criminal procedure, under which a judge, if so minded, might add a recommendation to mercy. Any such recommendation was almost invariably effective and it was after a long period of extreme anxiety that it was.

Chapter Thirteen
Kenya: The Unhappy Valley

Anyone leaving Uganda for Kenya in the mid nineteen fifties would have become aware of a marked change of atmosphere and environment. For one thing the countryside was, except in the far north, much more open and cultivated so that far less wild life was to be seen outside the Parks which were then in an early stage of development. The road from Uganda to Nairobi was then in poor to bad condition, though soon to be much improved. The Mau Mau Rebellion (against precisely what it has never been fully established) was coming to an end. What was particularly noticeable was that Africans in the townships, or passing on the roads, wore a surly disgruntled look in contrast to the frank easy smile that was to be encountered in most parts of Uganda.

All the land for many miles on either side of the road was given over to European settlers, the Africans having to be content with small holdings in restricted areas offering only a subsistence living. Many took service on European farms and ranches where they integrated happily enough with the families. Others found menial employment in local government, or in the few secondary industries existing at that time. But they still retained ownership of their land, and in many cases may well have nursed a resentment against the Europeans with their much larger holdings in exclusive locations. It has to be said however that when independence gave a chance of larger scale farming to some Africans, few were able to profit by it despite much practical help given by the settlers.

There can be no doubt that the presence of the settler, and the fruits of his labour, produced by far the best economic returns to the benefit of the overwhelming majority of the indigenous population, whatever their political feelings. Among sixty thousand Europeans in Kenya at the time of independence the settler was in the greatest numbers, doing the most work, taking the greater risks, providing the most wealth: and contributing considerably to the maintenance of law and order, and to the material benefit of the Africans.

The second most populous category were the civil servants, organised similarly to those in Uganda. Perhaps too many as already suggested, but those in the higher echelons were indispensible having regard to the general backwardness of the African at that time. Retirement from the service was obligatory at forty five when a few stayed on in the territory to make their homes in East Africa. The majority left so that apart from serving out a relatively short career they had no stake in the country. When independence came, somewhat unexpectedly, they went away with tidy pensions and handouts which was no doubt proper. In this respect the dispossessed settlers were not so fortunate, although they received reasonable compensation if their farms were bought up by Government under one or other of the schemes for the redistribution and resettlement of land in favour of the African. As it turned out, such schemes were by no means a success, certainly in the early years.

A third category of European expatriate consisted of professional and business men. Many large international companies maintained subsidiaries or agencies in the territories and their senior managements and staff were well provided for with housing, cars, home leave, entertainment allowances, pensions, and a measure of security as one might expect. But the individual entrepreneur enjoyed no such safety nets. Many were prosperous although there was no short cut to large fortunes; others found the going hard. There was no form of social security upon which they could fall back, and they had to pay for their own medical treatment in case of illness. This applied equally to the professionals: lawyers, doctors, accountants, and so on. Kenya was still in the nineteen fifties essentially a harsh pioneering country promoting an atmosphere of independence and cheerful expectations sometimes fulfilled: but it could be tough.

The main danger was the bottle. Situated in most areas, including Nairobi, at a height of over six thousand feet above sea level, and lying astride the equator, climatic conditions were more trying than one might think. Furthermore the environment tended to create among newcomers a feeling of relief from convention which affected their behaviour until they had had time to settle down to the more austere facts of life. But alcohol in that climate could be, and not infrequently was, a killer as those affected found it necessary in that enervating climate to 'top up' from the night before when the need to induce sleep had been met by over indulgence.

There was a professional man of high standing and outstanding ability who, finding himself through stress more and more addicted to the whisky, was in the habit of calling on his friends 'to help them out in case they had too much'. He usually found it convenient to stay until whatever bottle or decanter stood on the sideboard, however full it might be, was emptied. Being of excellent company he was usually welcome, but as consumption mounted it was deemed prudent, at one of his water holes, to limit the amount of the stuff available to about one third of a special bottle which was put out when noises outside indicated his imminent arrival.

One fine evening he was well installed when his host found it necessary to leave the room. On his return the whisky was not surprisingly finished which usually signalled the departure of the guest for other sources of supply. When his attention was drawn to the fact that there was no more whisky he announced: 'Oh yes there is. I have been out in the larder, and there is a full case there'. One could not win.

The particular charm and attraction of Kenya was the variety of interesting and amusing characters who had found their way there. This enabled people to make their own entertainment in what was a cultural desert. The were no art exhibitions, no visiting orchestras, and no historic buildings or monuments to be visited, although there was a theatre which provided good entertainment as well as a popular meeting place. The countryside, apart from its scenic attractions, was given over largely to game parks, but these were only developed after World War Two, now to become internationally popular.

Inevitably therefore the socially adventurous, and there were many, found their amusement in the exchange of hospitality and the membership of clubs. Comic relief was sometimes provided by the antics of some members of an eccentric society. There was a story involving two well known such members of Irish extraction. One evening they went, with two pieces of 'homework', to a restaurant about ten miles out of town where they all dined well if not altogether wisely. On the way home almost inevitably a quarrel broke out, possibly brought on by the presence of female company. The driver stopped the car on a lonely stretch of road when both men got out. After a few skirmishes the driver punched the other on his Hibernian conk. This caused him to sit down heavily in a cowpat, carelessly left on the road by a Boran cow. The driver then took off at top speed, complete with the two girls, back to Nairobi.

The place where this happened was in Kikuyu territory: no place to be at three in the morning in those stirring times. It was high up, at about eight thousand feet and freezing cold. The seat of our hero's trousers was covered in 'merde', his nose was bleeding profusely, and there was no way he could conveniently get anywhere. He was up that proverbial creek. It then occurred to him that some three miles down the road there was a railway station where he could jump the train from Uganda, due to pass through early in the morning. There might also be shelter from the nagging wind. He ran. The station was closed but he managed to find refuge in a telephone kiosk where he sat on the floor and dozed off.

He awoke to the sound of the clanking of wheels. Leaping aboard a first class coach he opened a carriage door and with no mean relief clambered in. It seems that an Asian gentleman occupying a seat in the far corner of the compartment took one look at the blood stained apparition, and departed through the other door to who knows what fate. Arrival at Nairobi station was something of an event. No taxi driver was prepared to take him as fare, so that he was forced to proceed to his home on foot, pursued by a jeering mob.

Markets in manufactured goods were at that time in East Africa much too limited to support much by way of secondary industry, and the high relative cost of local production excluded any export trade in such goods. The greater volume of consumer goods had to be imported, Britain enjoying a somewhat priveleged position in this respect, but by no means a monopoly. It follows that many of the business houses in Nairobi were import agencies which distributed goods to wholesalers, usually Asians, who sold on to small traders situated in the townships throughout the territories. The need for industrial development in order to achieve a balanced distribution of labour and the development of managerial and technical skills and enterprise among Africans, thus providing the nucleus of a middle class, as well as to replace imports and thus achieve some degree of self-sufficiency for the territories was of greater importance than many colonial officials recognised, or perhaps cared to.

The basic difficulties, in addition to market shortages, lay in the lack of skilled and semi-skilled manpower and of the availability locally of raw materials, most of which had to be imported at an uneconomic cost. All the essential infrastructure was there from which thriving mixed economy might have been developed: docks and harbours at Mombasa and Dar es Salaam; an efficient railway network covering a substantial part of the territories; in some places good, and in others passable roads. Electrical power was available from the Owen Falls project, albeit expensive pending a much wider takeoff. Any viable project could attract capital and management expertise, either locally or from overseas.

The first incursion by Europeans into Kenya took place in eighteen eighty one when Lord Delamere carried out his first exploratory visit, the purpose being to establish whether the country was fit for settlement by white men. The party marched for many days through the Highlands without encountering any Africans. Inter-tribal strife and small pox, among other epidemics had all but wiped them out. The later arrival of the settlers in large numbers brought about a rapid improvement in the lot of many Africans with resulting increase in population. By the mid nineteen fifties there were some six million inhabitants of Kenya; five million in Uganda; and twelve million spread across the much larger territory of Tanganyika.

The great majority of Africans were engaged in small scale farming. To try to turn enough of them into industrial workers was a daunting task requiring patience and planning. An aptitude testing unit set up at about that time for the purpose of carrying out scientific tests aimed at assessing the physical and common-sense adoptability of individual workers for the various tasks needing to be done in a given industry would allot marks after three days of trials. Gradings started at zero and moved upwards to plus five, or downwards to minus five. Of those tested most Europeans finished up in the plus two to plus five range; Africans almost invariably minus two to minus five. This led to very high wastage of materials; breakdowns of machinery owing to clumsy handling; a high proportion of 'seconds', and so on giving rise to greatly increased operating costs. Added to all this was bad timekeeping and absenteeism, often the result of habitual week-end drunkenness.

It was estimated that, in the textile industry, in the nineteen fifties, one Lancashire worker could alone operate twenty looms; a Japanese could manage six; and that it took two African workers to operate only one. In the face of such evidence the view, held by many, might be justified that the Ricardian theory of division of labour should be allowed to prevail under which the employment of workers in tasks not fully suited to their skills, or lack of them, is uneconomic, and that on this analogy the manufacturing function should be reserved to those best qualified to carry it out at the lowest cost. This meant that the African should be left to devote his time and energy to basic agriculture, thus condemning him to permanent peasantry and subservience, leading to idleness and waste.

This theory ignores the need for Africa to develop a strong and sophisticated middle class capable of filling management and professional voids, and thereby keeping inequalities under control. It is only thus that a developing country can settle down to the prospect of long term prosperity, and this can only be achieved by a substantial broadening of practical education and training, particularly in the industrial and related fields.

Those in East Africa in the early fifties whose task it was to promote this development were well aware of the difficulties and limitations as outlined. These were not always appreciated or catered for by officialdom. Nevertheless since the end of World War Two great strides had been made by entrepreneurs ready to pit their endeavours against sometimes negative attitudes. Companies were set up locally for the production of sugar, cotton and synthetic textiles, beer, glass, metal boxes, building steel; and for the construction and management of hotels and other tourist aids. This and the general improvement in agricultural prosperity gave encouragement to the inflow of professional services: bankers, lawyers, doctors, accountants and the like: inspired by the new and challenging environment.

All this was brought to an end by the home government announcement that early independence was intended and that full political power was to be transferred to an all-African administration without the participation of the white settler. This news came in about nineteen sixty and resulted in upheaval throughout the territory. In some cases farms and businesses were closed down and abandoned, and many professional men left. There were few Africans with the necessary training to enable them to fill the vacancies left by the Asians and Europeans, but this fact was ignored by home politicians greedy for a complete break with the past.

It was clearly fitting as well as of great practical importance that from the start the white settler should have been involved in the change. As things stood they were to have no valid representation while providing, together with the Asians, by far the greater share of the revenue. Many had invested their modest all in the country. Many could point to the fact that they represented the third and even fourth generation of their family to have contributed to the relatively short life of the colony. Through determination and massive hard work they had survived the early heartbreaks attendant on the setting up of farmlands: coping with little known crop and cattle diseases, the depredations of tribal forays and of wild animals, and the vagaries of international markets.

Only shortly before this the settlers had been faced by the sinister activities of the Mau Mau movement which led to the death of thousands of loyal Africans, and the true significance of which seems never to have been fully established. In coping with this and its constant danger the white farmers had exhibited that degree of hardihood so characteristic of their race.

As to the loyalty of the African population, there can be little doubt that the majority of the peasantry who were not indifferent through ignorance were tolerant of white rule, and not blind to its benefits.

There was a story at that time of one of the many highly respected tribal chiefs who was asked whether he would prefer to be ruled by a black government. He thought for a long time, spat, and then asked: 'Is there a Governor in Nairobi?'; the answer came: 'Yes'; 'Is he paid to do the work?' Answer again: 'Yes'. 'Then why does he not get on with it and leave us alone?' Propaganda, maybe. Truth, not unlikely.

It was against this background that a senior British Minister on a visit to the colony saw fit, on arrival in Nairobi and being faced by a deputation of long term and highly responsible European farmers requesting talks, to announce that he saw no reason for discussion with a 'handful of white settlers'. We all know now where that has since led.

Appendices

Interview with Lt. Col. Patrick Hearn (Ret)
*by Sue Farrington at Hearn's home in
Oxford on 23rd September, 1999*

Family connections with India.
Started in 1824 with General Thomas McGowan who was Patrick Hearn's Great Grandfather, a Scottish lawyer who took service with the East Indian Co. and rose to become Judge Advocate. He was a General in the Madras Army in India. His nickname was "Certainly Not", as that was all he ever said. When asked why he had this name he said if you say "No" you can always change your mind. If you say "Yes" you can never change your mind. This shows a standard of integrity and strictness of truth and propriety that caused us to be able to run a huge country with vast populations with only about 2000 administrators all selected from the highest available people from universities.

General McGowan's daughter (my grandmother) was only 16 when she brought him home to Marseille where he died and was buried in the English cemetery in Marseille. She married my grandfather Charles Hearn a Wykehamist scholar. He married late in life and had three children, one died, one of which was Col Sir Gordon Hearn, my father. Grandfather Charles Hearn established the Imperial Police Force. He served in the Madras Staff Core. He was a Winchester scholar. These were the sorts of people who went out to India. He died young and his wife (my grandmother) became a widow for 55 years. He was awarded the Bravery of Service. This was the price you paid for Indian service but it was something everyone felt was well worthwhile, partly because of the country and challenges but also because of the people.

In 1891 my father, Gordon, also a Winchester scholar, went to India on the Frontier Bombay. At the turn of the Century the Indian Railways were surveyed. General Wilcocks, an Australian, felt that a railway should be built. (The 1906 War against tribes was called Wilcocks week-end War.)

My father in France CRE three and a half years with the 9th Scottish Division, was promoted to full Colonel and transferred to the Australian 3rd Core as Assistant Engineer. After the war Field Marshall Birdwood in Australia asked Gordon to build the Khyber railway in India as there was no future in a previously built but failed railway, that had to be ripped up.

This took 5 years. He drew up the plans that were adopted. The planning and direction took 3 years, then the track was laid to the Afghan border. He was knighted for his direction of the railway. He then left and went to Bengal to become the Managing Director of Eastern Bengal Railways. He retired and came home to England to live for another 25 years. He married the daughter of the Hallowell Carew family and they had 3 children (one died). I was the third child. I was born in Arcola, Madras. At that time my father was the Chief Inspector of Railways.

My father was born in Madras in 1871. He had a sister and a younger brother who didn't serve in India. His eldest son Charles died 2 or 3 years ago. He emigrated to Australia and he was in the Royal Australian Airforce and left a son and daughter whom I know, both very successful. I was the third child, as the one in between died as happened in those days.

I attended Bradfield School and then went on to Grenoble University in France as my father felt this would be good for a commercial career. I studied Economics and a smattering of Law. However when I returned to England nobody wanted to employ me because I had read Economics which in those days was thought to be politically subversive. Also, a French University was looked down upon in those days. I therefore joined the army as a private soldier in England for 18 months which was a fine experience. I got to know the English working men who were fine, decent, honest soldiers with plenty of common sense. While there I won the Bisley team cup young soldiers prize. This achievement helped me to get into Sandhurst together with my family record which helped. I also had 4 blues in rugger, shooting, hockey and athletics, and I won the economic history prize.

1936-1941 I was in India. Our regiment, the Frontier Force Rifles, was sent to the Middle East, Syria and then on to North Africa. I was in Staff College in India and I married a Nicholson. Her Great Uncle was the famous John Nicholson. My wife was a staunch, tough, only white woman ever to live in the Khyber before or since, where I was commanding and so we had a quarter there.

I went from Staff College, Burma 39th Indian Division, then posted to Chindits under the command of Brigadier Major Calvert with whom incidentally I had been at school. It was a tough but happy year. Then back to my regiment commanded after Armistice when Japs surrendered. I was then posted back to India and to my regiment and commanded the regimental centre in Abbotabad during the changeover. I had 5,000 men there. After two years in command I decided to go back to home to the UK. I had three children born in India (Limbdi, Abbottabad and Mussourie). However, Sir Ambrose Dundas asked me to take over the Khyber and command it and I couldn't resist the idea — I took my wife and children with me. I heard later that the tribes there were proud that I trusted them with my family. They had a lovely spirit and attitude.

We returned home to the UK in 1950. I was awarded the Pakistan Independence Medal which was pure silver on a ribbon. I wear it with considerable pride. If we had stayed on my children would be living and working in India, probably in the Indian Civil Service.

My eldest son has a PhD in Biology and he is the Director of the RSB in Canberra. My second son has a PhD in Economics and is presently the Permanent Secretary in the Ministry of Natural Resources. I have a daughter in New Zealand married to a New Zealander, a very good chap, and they will shortly join the others in Canberra. I shall therefore have three children and nine grandchildren over there in Canberra, all part of the Commonwealth still.

After I returned to England I was called to the bar in 1952. I wanted to build a career as a barrister but unfortunately I ran out of money, so I had to seek employment as an economist which I did in the brewing industry. The Colonial Office offered me a senior post in the Ugandan Government as an Economist in 1955 and I stayed until 1957, with responsibility for sitting on various central committees for the whole of East Africa. Uganda already had its own parliament and Kabaka (king) so there was a smooth transition to independence. In Kenya there were no arrangements to hand over the running of the country to people who had had a chance to be trained as high level administrators.

India trained their own engineers way back, so by the time independence came the light was the railways. When I was leaving for India my father said you won't make a career there as they are going to break up, and the Indian is a jolly fine fellow. Leadership family Budras — he sent me.

The African was not as educated as the Indian had been. East Africa was settled in 1890, which did not give enough time to develop the African. If I may make some criticism, far too many menial jobs were held by Europeans that could have been held by Africans and the troubles taken place since, might never have happened. Indians as well as Africans were excluded from jobs that Europeans took over. A lot of the Indians were highly intelligent, especially in Uganda. There were several big Indian Industrialists, for example the Madhvani's whom I would like to mention because of their outstanding contribution to East Africa. Muljibhai Madhvani had gone to Africa as a clerk on the railways. He died with 20 million at least. He started growing sugar. I helped him by getting the Government to award him much more land. He had 13,000 acres to start up with a factory and large amount of employment with a great deal of training available. I was in charge of portofolio of industrial development which suited me very much. As the Senior Assistant Secretary in the Ministry of Commerce and Industry I introduced innovations. I was able to save the cotton industry which was British run. They had to pay import duty on the raw material. I did not think this was right. I managed to get the Government to agree to take it off altogether. If I do this you need to invest more money. Put up price of sugar which was contracted and said to Madhvani you invest more. Madhvani was unassuming — a Hindu. He first asked me to breakfast. In the course of talking when I told him my eldest son was born in Limbdi, he was astonished. When I went into practice in Kenya which I did eventually, he employed me as his lawyer. That was very lucrative and gave me a great start.

His son Jayant was a go getter with projects with the Nile Brewery, Battlebox Co., Construction Steel Co. and Glass Bottle Co. for which there was plenty of demand for we had the raw materials. Sadly he died at age 49 of a heart attack in India which was a great loss to the business community in East Africa let alone India, because he had a textile factory in Bombay and then started a factory in Jinja, Uganda. I raised money with the World Bank in order to help in 1957, pre independence, which came in 1962. I only had a three year contract. I was 45 when I was offered a partnership in a firm in Nairobi. Nairobi had good schools. All my 3 sons went to St Mary's, run by the Holy Ghost Fathers from Dublin which is an offshoot of Black Rock, Dublin. I had three sons and two daughters. My youngest son is Managing Director of Morgans Bank in London — my eldest daughter is in Southampton. She has done very well too. She has taken retirement as an Assistant Principal at the University due to the political interference in the teaching sector and she has now reverted to teaching again at a private Catholic School which makes her much happier. I told my children what you want in life is not so much money but happiness. You can have that and they got the money too!

I went to Kenya in 1957 and did a year or so in partnership. I then set up on my own running a court practice and also an industrial business development practice as an economist. This built up into a substantial business. When change in Africa came I felt it would be best for my children to go to England.

I got my children home to England to go to university. All enjoyed school and went to various universities and all got very good degrees. I joined the Treasury where I was Instructing Solicitor for the Crown from 1969-1973. For two and a half years I worked on a big case for them with six months in court with a panel of 5 judges. This involved more economics than law.

After that when I was 56 I was head hunted and became the Legal Director in the Reed Group for 10 years. They dealt in wall paper and paint and general decorative products. I travelled 74 times around, Europe, Asia, and the States. I began to feel the strain and I succumbed to illness when I developed Polymyalgia as a result of the stress. I went to Spain with my wife and I recovered after a couple of years. At around age 67 I started writing books. About 1981 I started writing. While in Spain I wrote a book on the "Practicalities of entering into Commercial Contracts" which sold extremely well until my Publisher was taken over by a bigger Publisher and everything stopped.

However, I got a letter from the Foreign Office to say my book had been translated into Chinese. However the Chinese do not pay Royalties. I went on to write on "Licensing Industrial Property" on patents, trademarks and industrial designs which went into a second edition. I then wrote "International Business Agreements" which sets out model Agreements on various things like agencies, distributor ships, licensing of patents — this opens the eyes to licensing models which can be used by people entering law. The next one I wrote was "After Maastricht" doing business in the single market and its effect on industry. That didn't go as expected as it was given to the wrong publishers, but I will take these to Australia with me so they might find a home there. So much work can be done in these fields, and my experience I had in these fields needs to be left behind for other people to profit from. I also wrote a book about India called "Stupendous Anomaly".

During my travels I met many businessmen who said how on earth did a country of your size and in those days, manage to take over India and rule so effectively for so many years. The Germans were particularly interested. I explained that, unlike other nations that had colonies, we were always careful to select the cream of our people, for example George Cunningham, the Governor, is well known on the frontier of India to this day. He had an excellent career and was Captain of rugger at Oxford, then Captain of Scotland at rugger. He achieved a first in the ICS exam nations, a double first at Oxford and won the British Amateur Open Championship at golf. That was the sort of man who was sent to India. Both my father and grandfather who were Wykehamist scholars, had a high degree of intellect such as The Foreign Office or Home Civil Service needed a high degree of intellect. You had to get a feeling for Hindu, which was not easy to come to grips with, and of course Muslim. Numbers of zappas who served in India were quite remarkable. They also won a number of VCs, including Elren a cousin of mine who won a VC at Detral.

My grandfather, Col. Charles Shuckburgh Hearn was Inspector General of the Madras Police. He accompanied and entertained Edward VII on his famous visit to India when he was Prince of Wales. They got on well and grandfather got a CIE apart from other medals. When Edward left he gave my grandfather a riding switch from Aspreys in Mount Street. It was gold from top to bottom and the top handle had the Royal Arms. This switch was inherited by my brother Charles when my father died. I sent it out to him in Australia. When my grandfather was seriously ill, living at that time in Hove, Edward, who was still the Prince of Wales, sent him a letter saying he remembered him very well from India. He was sorry to learn of his illness and he would send him some game from Sandringham in the hope that he would get better.

My father was against me going to India. He knew things could not go on and we had to hand over power. There was no intention then that I should go to India. In the end I did go to India.

Col Patrick Hearn at his home near Oxford on 23rd September 1999, shortly before he departed for Australia.

A Game of Marbles In The Khyber Pass
by Cynthia Hearn

Introduction

Cynthia Hearn (nee Nicholson) came from a family that had served in India since 1810, including Brigadier General John Nicholson, the "Hero of Delhi". She grew up in India, went to "finish" in London and Geneva and met and married Patrick Hearn in December 1940. The fox terrier Susie, seen in Figure 9, belonged to Pat and he asked Cynthia to look after her when his regiment went to fight in Syria and Iraq. The dog kept their link, and later in 1943 averted a kidnap attempt in Limbdi on son John. Cynthia followed the flag, was totally devoted to her husband and children – who she supported in creating many calm and secure homes in India and Pakistan, England, Uganda, and Kenya. Her status as an army wife demanded leadership under threat. While educated sporadically in the way of the time, she later taught French in English high schools, and was elected a member of MENSA. This article is about all she wrote – but we include it as a unique view from the Khyber. Her presence with the children gave great strength to Patrick, as a sign of his trust in the warriors around him.

A Game of Marbles in the Khyber Pass

Mention of the Khyber Pass conjures up a picture of grim and austere hills inhabited by fierce and warlike tribesmen whose favourite occupation, when not fighting each other - family and tribal feuds to the death are part of their lives — would seem to be sniping at the troops whose duty it is to guard the pass with its road and railway; or to raid villages in the plains in search of loot. Indeed for many centuries, at least up to the time the British left the country, this was a true picture.

The Pass is a principal gateway between Pakistan and Afghanistan, and its defence against the possibility of external invasion is of great strategic importance. Thus the guardianship of the Pass is no easy task. Primarily this is the duty of the famous Khyber Rifles, of which the men are recruited from among the very tribesmen here mentioned, and which keeps manned and ready the various posts situated at tactical points throughout the twenty seven miles of rugged mountainous country through which the road passes. From these posts frequent patrols are sent out to scour the countryside in search of information and sometimes trouble. Many times in the history of the Pass the tribes have combined to launch major attacks on its defenders principally from the Tirah, a range of broken and forbidding hills flanking it to the South where most of them live in remote fortified villages, and where visitors are strictly forbidden to go.

I would like to describe briefly the life of an English family, our family, living at Landi Kotal, the fort at the head of the Khyber Pass shortly after the partition of India and the creation of Pakistan. Up to this time the tribesmen had always been hostile towards the British, but at the time of which I am relating they were supposedly more friendly as the Government was now in the hands of their own co-religists. At this time my husband, a regular officer in the British Indian Army, was sent to command the Khyber Rifles. Owing to the apparently improved relations, permission was given for the families of officers to live with their husbands at Landi Kotal, where there was adequate accommodation. Thus it was that, amid great excitement among our three children, we made the move up to the fort. I believe that ours were the first English children, and probably the last, to have lived there. The memory of the six months or so during which we stayed is somewhat dim to them now as John, the eldest, was only six years old at the time, Susan being five. The youngest, Simon, then twelve months old, has of course no recollection of it at all.

The country around Landi Kotal is arid and bleak, but the hills have a fascination of their own, and one gets a feeling of exhilaration in the crisp air on fine winter mornings with the sun shining brightly and with a fine view of the snow covered mountains of the Hindu Khush far to the North. But it was a bit alarming to know that in these hills there lived such potentially dangerous people, whose gun was an essential part of their equipment, more important to them than food or clothes, as they must be prepared to defend themselves against attack or to relieve occasional boredom by shooting up the troops, not so much through hostility as part of their way of life. Thus in spite of the overt friendliness the entire frontier still has to be guarded by the Pakistan Army.

Life in the Pass was interesting as a change from the normal army environment. We went down to Peshawar at the foot of the Pass for an occasional party. At one point on the road, carved into the rocks, could be seen the different badges of British regiments which had at one time or another served in the Pass which the tribesmen sometimes amused themselves by using for target practice, a particular favourite for their attention being the "running boy": the naked Hermes, messenger of the gods, emblem of the Royal Corps of Signals! The children were fond of dressing up and playing at tribesmen and soldiers. It was all very strange and exciting for them at first. There was a very large area inside the fort where they could wander at will, and were quite safe, as the great gates were always kept shut and manned by an armed guard while sentries were posted in towers all round.

On our first morning in the Khyber John could not be found, but we were not unduly perturbed as we knew he must be safe inside the walls and that he must have gone off to do a bit of exploring on his own. After searching for some time we found him at the front gate where we had not thought to look. He had wandered up to the gate and, feeling a little uncertain at the sight of the armed guard on duty, he had felt in his pocket for the comfort of his familiar and well-used marbles. He commenced to play with them on the ground, a proceeding which increasingly fascinated the guard who, after watching for a bit, and with encouragement by signs from John, slung his rifle and proceeded to join in the game. When discovered they were absorbed in what they were doing. Kipling's statement that "East is East, and West is West, and never the twain shall meet" did not here apply for both had met in complete understanding - over a game of marbles! Of course guards are not posted for that purpose, especially in the Khyber, and disciplinary action had to be taken, although I understood that in the special circumstances of the case he got nothing worse than a sound ticking off.

Living in the fort enabled us to meet some important and interesting people, as everyone visiting the Frontier wanted to see the famous Khyber Pass and the nearby border with Afghanistan. Anthony Eden came, also the Prince de Ligne of the Belgian royal family, leading a delegation. They had tea in the Officers Mess. Several other VIPs turned up while we were there. A picturesque sight were the camel caravans which passed through on their way to Peshawar and far beyond, taking with them beautiful Persian carpets and Afghan ponies among other things. Many a British officer has come home with fine Eastern carpets which they have picked up very cheaply from these Afghans, and which would have cost a great deal of money in this country.

On the whole it was a pleasant experience, but after six months of looking out on the bleak mountain landscape I was not sorry once more to see the green fields of England and to get back to what one thought, perhaps mistakenly, to be civilisation. As my husband was the last British commander of the Khyber Rifles, our sojourn in the Pass was, I now feel, unique and a bit of history.

LTCOL Hugh Patrick Hearn: Medals

Figure 19: Pat's Medals, Mounted

Cynthia and Patrick Hearn: Headstone, Southampton

Figure 20: In Peace – Chandlers Ford Cemetery, Southampton

Editors

John Patrick Hearn (eldest son)

John Hearn was destined for the army from an early age (see Figure 11, the 6-year old in the background). Thanks to the 150-year military service of the family, he grew up in peace, choosing a career as a scientist and professor. But the international imperative of the family genes run strong, as he served in senior positions in five top global universities in Ireland, Scotland, England, the US, and Australia.

He published 230 scientific articles and six edited books in human and animal fertility, stem cell science, and higher education reform. He led international university research networks in environment, agriculture and food, public health, education, and economic development; and emphasised the development of early career researchers.

He was an adviser to governments, universities, and international agencies. John and Margaret (nee McNair) rejoiced in their daughter, four sons and nine grandchildren, and alternated between homes in Sydney and London. John passed away in Sydney on 1st November 2024.

Gordon Bruce Hearn (eldest nephew)

Gordon Hearn graduated as an engineer in communications and industrial electronics and worked in television broadcasting in Perth, Western Australia. He was then attracted to the booming aviation industry in that state and worked for 18 years there with the Civil Aviation Authority, finishing his stay there as chief engineer. He obtained his pilot's licence and used a company aircraft for his travel around Western Australia – the western third of the country.

He moved to Canberra to work on the modernisation program for the Australian airways system before starting a systems engineering consultancy business servicing government and industry engineering projects; a large part of this work was defence-related.

After rapid growth of the business demanding large capital investment, Gordon and his partners decided to sell the business to an American corporation, before sampling partial retirement and moving to Noosa. Not wishing to stop altogether, he continued working part-time until 2021.

Index

A

Abbott, James, 56
Abbottabad, 5, 51
Afghanistan, 16, 67-68, 71, 73, 80
    invasion of, 67, 73, 84
    Second Afghan War, 75, 80
Afridi tribe, 70, 71, 80-82, 83, 86, 87
Africa, East, 5, 8, 160
Ahmadzai operation (1940), 85
Alexander, Field Marshal, 70
Alexander the Great, 69
Ambela campaign (1863), 74-75, 79
Army
    British Army, 5, 64, 65, 85-86
    Indian Army, 5, 56, 65-66, 78, 83-84, 88-90
Ascot, 24
Asquith, Herbert Henry, 18, 19, 20
Auchinleck, Field Marshal, 70
Australia, 5, 8, 11, 48, 50
Aylmer, Fenton, Capt., 77

B

Bader, Douglas, 5
Baden Baden, 24
Bajaur, 69
Baluchistan, 67
Bangash tribe, 70
Bannerman, Sir Henry Campbell, 18
Bannu, 56, 70, 71, 79, 85
Barristers, 5, 51-52
Battles
    Chillianwala (Rassul), 60-61, 62
    Gujerat, 61
    Meeanee, 61
    Ramnagar, 59-60
Beecham, Thomas, Sir, 17
Belloc, Hilaire, 17, 21
Bengal Lancers, 79
Berry Brothers & Rudd, 27
Bikanir Camel Corps, 66
Blood, Bindon, Gen. Sir, 79, 80
Boisragon, Lieut., 77
Bradfield School, 5
British Empire, 8, 16, 72
Buner, 69, 74
Burma, 5
Burma Rifles, 66
Burns, John, 18
Byron, Lord, 26

C

Calcutta Light Horse, 66
Campaigns
    Ambela (1863), 74-75, 79
    Chitral Relief (1895), 77-78
    Hunza-Nagar (1891), 76-77
    Ipi (1936), 85
    Mohmand (1933), 85
    Mohmand (1897), 80
    Tirah Expedition (1897), 80-82
    Second Afghan War
        (1878), 75, 80
    Second Sikh War (1848-
        49), 59-63, 67, 68
Cawnpore, 63
Chakdara Fort, 79
Chaliapin, Feodor, 17
Chalt, 76
Chamber pots, 43
Chesterton, G. K., 17
Chindit Brigade (77th), 5
Chitral, 69, 77-78
Churchill, Winston, 18, 36, 64,
    79, 167
Clubs (London), 25, 27
    Boodles, 27
    Brooks, 27
    White's, 27
Coq au vin, 36, 37
Corps of Guides, 56, 79
Cowes, 24
Cricket, 43
Crimea, 16
Cromwell Road, 25

D

Dalhousie, Earl of, 58, 63
Dargai heights, 81
Delhi, 50, 57, 63, 72
Derby, The, 24
Dehra Ismail Khan (DIK), 71
Diaghelev, Sergei, 17
Dir, 69
Dost Mohammed, Amir, 67, 68, 73
Dover, 33
Durand, Lieut. Colonel, 76

E

Earls Court, 23
Edward VII, King, 16, 20
Edwardes, Herbert, 56, 58
Edwardian era, 17
Egyptians (cigarettes), 26
Elgar, Edward, Sir, 17
End of Empire, 8
England, 8, 18, 48, 50, 51, 64, 67,
    94, 96, 97 159, 168, 186, 198,
    199, 200, 203, 206, 210, 213

F

Fakir, 85
Fortnum & Masons, 25, 26
France, 5, 12, 29, 32-47, 65, 78
Free French Army, 38, 39
Fribourg & Treyer, 26
Frontier Force Rifles
    (5th/13th), 5, 50, 52
Frontier medals, 86
Frontier Scouts, 66

G

Galsworthy, John, 17
Gandamak, Treaty of (1879), 80
Gandhi (Ghandi), 50
General Strike (1926), 21
Germany, 20, 39, 46, 72
Gilbert, William, Sir, 62
Gilgit, 76, 78
Gladstone, William Ewart, 26
Gordon Highlanders, 81
Gough, Hugh, Gen. Lord,
    59, 60, 61, 62
Gray's Inn, 5, 51
Great Crash (1929), 15, 46, 48
Great War (WWI), 7, 15, 29,
    31, 46, 50, 64, 77, 83, 84
Greeks (ancient), 70
Grenoble, France, 5, 7, 12, 32
Grey, Edward, Sir, 18
Gujerat, Battle of, 61
Gurkhas (5th), 77
Gwynne, Nell, 26

H

Haldane, Richard, 18
Hardinge, Henry, Lord, 58
Hatchard's (bookshop), 26
Hazara, 56
Hearn, Charles (brother),
    12, 24 (ref to), 50
Hearn, Cynthia (née Nicholson,
    wife), 5, 8, 10, 52, 53, 54, 50
Hearn, Gordon, Col. Sir (father), 50
Hearn, Hugh Patrick,
    Lieut. Col. (author)
        birth, 5, 7
    career phases, 7-8, 50-52
    children, 5, 8, 10, 52
    education, 5, 7, 12,
        13, 32-47, 50
    legal career, 5, 8, 51-52
    marriage, 5, 50, 54
    medals, 10, 21, 211
    military service, 5, 7, 13,
        50-51, 52, 55, 66-90
    retirement, 5, 8
    writings, 5, 8, 10, 163
Henley, 24
Himalayas, 76
Hindustani Fanatics, 74
Hitler, Adolf, 39, 72
Home Rule (Ireland), 21
Hunza-Nagar expedi-
    tion (1891), 76-77, 78
Hyderabad, India, 5

I

India, 5, 7, 8, 16, 49-90
    1857 Mutiny, 50, 57,
        63, 72-73, 83
    British rule in, 8, 50-51,
        56-63, 67-90
    Independence/
        Partition, 8, 50-51
    North West Frontier, 5,
        16, 50, 52, 64-90
    service conditions, 85-90
Indian Army. See Army, Indian
Indian Civil Service (ICS), 50
Indus River, 67, 68, 71
Iraq, 5
Ireland, 21, 51, 57

J

Jacksons of Piccadilly, 26
Jalalabad, 67
Jamrud, 86
Jhelum River, 60, 62
Jinja, Uganda, 161
Jinnah, Muhammad Ali, 50

K

Kabul, 67, 68
Karsovina, Tamara, 17
Kelly, J.G., Col., 78
Kenya, 5, 7, 8, 157, 160, 187-194
Khattaks tribe, 70
Khyber Pass, 50, 51, 55, 62, 67, 69, 70, 75, 80, 81, 84, 86, 87
Khyber Rifles, 5, 8, 51, 55, 80, 87
Kipling, Rudyard, 52
Kohat, 70, 71, 81
Koh-i-Nur diamond, 62-63
Kurram valley, 69, 70, 75, 84

L

Labour Party, 18, 21, 50
Lahore, 59, 67
Landi Kotal, 51, 55, 71, 80, 84, 87
Lawrence, Henry, Sir, 56, 61
Lawrence, John, 63
Liberal Party, 18, 21
Lisburn, Northern Ireland, 57
Lloyd, Marie, 17
Lloyd George, David, 18, 19, 20, 21
Lobb (bootmakers), 27
Lock (hatters), 27
Lockhart, William, Sir, 81, 87

London, 5, 11, 16, 23, 24, 25-27, 48, 160
Lords, House of, 19, 21
Lords (cricket ground), 24
Low, Robert, Sir, 77
Lucknow, 63
Lumsden, Harry, 56

M

Macaulay, Thomas Babington, 26
Mackeson, Frederick, 56
Macmillan, Harold, 8
Mahsud tribe, 69, 71, 83, 84
Malakand Pass, 69, 71, 77, 79, 80
Marie Louise (cook), 36-37
Maurice (professor), 32-36, 37-38
Maugham, W. Somerset, 17
Melbourne, Lord, 26
Mess (officers'), 64, 89
Midjourney (AI), Ref to concept
Mill, John Stuart, 19
Millais, John Everett, Sir, 17
Mohmand tribe, 70, 80, 83, 85
Morley, John, 18
Mountbatten, Lord Louis, 8, 50, 51
Mullahs, 77, 80
Multan, 58-59, 60, 61
Music halls, 17, 29-30

N

Nagar, 76, 77
Napier, Charles, Sir, 61
Nehru, Jawaharlal, 50
Nicholson, Cynthia. See Hearn, Cynthia

Nicholson, John, Brig. Gen. ("Hero of Delhi"), 50, 57, 73
Nicholson, John, OBE (father-in-law), 5, 50
Nijinsky, Vaslav, 17
Nilt, fortress of, 77
North West Frontier Province (NWFP), 5, 16, 50, 52, 64-90
    campaigns, 74-84
    description, 68-71
    history, 67-68, 72-73
    service conditions, 85-90
    tribes, 68-71 (See also individual tribes)

O

Old age pensions, 18
Orakzai tribe, 70, 80, 81
Osama Bin Laden, 51
Outposts (frontier), 89
Oxford University, 33

P

Pakistan, 5, 7, 8, 50-51
Pall Mall, 26
Pathans, 68, 69, 70, 73, 75, 77, 79, 88
Pavlova, Anna, 17
Peiwar Kotal, 75
Persia (Iran), 33, 39, 68
Peshawar, 56, 57, 68, 70, 71, 80, 82, 86
Piccadilly, 25, 26
Picquets (military), 74, 75, 82
Politicos (administrators), 56-63
Pollock, George, Gen. Sir, 68, 87
Ports (wine), 15
Poverty, 16, 18, 19
Punjab, 58, 63, 67, 68, 72
    annexation of, 62, 68
Punjabi Mussalmans, 88

Q

Queen Victoria, 16, 87
Quetta, 5

R

Racine, Jean, 34
Rajputs (Logra), 88
Ramnagar, Battle of, 59-60
Ranjeet Singh, 62
Rats, Les (rugby club), 40
Razmak, 71, 72, 84, 85
Regent's Park, 48
Regent Street, 26, 49
Ritz Hotel (London), 25
Roberts, Frederick, Lord, 56, 57
Robey, George, Sir, 17
Royal Academy, 26
Royal Engineers, 23, 50, 77
Royal Corps of Signals, 86
Rugby, 39-40
Russia, 56, 67

S

Sam Browne, Gen. Sir, 87
Sandhurst Military Academy, 5, 7, 13, 50, 64, 65
Sandringham, 16
Sarajevo, 27
Sargent, John Singer, 17

Schools
    Bradfield School, 5
    Prep schools, 32
    Public schools, 32, 39, 46
    Temple Grove Preparatory School, 5
Scott's (restaurant), 26
Sebastian-Smith, Charles Arthur, Major ("Bassy"), 23-31
Second World War (WWII), 7, 15, 50, 79, 83, 85
Sepoys, 73, 74, 88-89
Shah Sujah, 62
Shandur Pass, 78
Shaw, George Bernard, 17
Shere Singh, Gen., 59, 60, 61, 62
Shikar (hunting), 137 (Chapter title only in TOC)
Shropshire, 23, 29
Sickert, Walter, 17
Sikhs, 58, 59-63, 67, 68, 73, 79, 86, 88, 89
    Second Sikh War, 59-63, 67, 68
Sind, 61
Snuff, 26
South Africa, 8, 16, 48
Southampton, 10, 11, 212
St James's Church, 26
St James's Palace, 26
St James's Street, 25, 26-27
Stilton cheese, 25
Strasbourg Pie, 25
Students, 7, 32-47
Subedar/Subedar Major, 88, 90
Suffragettes, 21

Swat, 69, 74, 77, 79
Syria, 5, 38

T

Taurus Express, 38
Temple Grove Preparatory School, 5
Territorial Army/Forces, 48, 66, 83
Tirah, 69, 70, 80-82
    Expeditionary Force (1897), 80-82, 87
Tobacco, 19, 26
Tochi Valley, 79
Trade Disputes Act (1906), 18
Trade Unions, 18, 21
Transport Workers' strike (1911), 21
Treasury Solicitors, 5
Trotter, Lionel James, 57
Turis tribe, 70
Turkey, 38
Turkomans, 56

U

Uganda, 5, 7, 8, 52, 157, 160, 161, 164-184
Ulster, 21
Umra Khan, 77
Unemployment, 15, 18, 19, 46, 48
United Kingdom (UK), 5, 8, 48
    (See also Britain, England)
Universities
    French, 32-47
    Grenoble, 5, 7, 12, 32-47
    Oxford, 33
Urdu language, 89
Yusufzai tribe, 69, 74, 83

V

Vaughan Williams, Ralph, 17
Viceroy's Commissioned Officers (VCOs), 88, 89
Vichy, 24
Victoria Cross (VC), 77
Victoria, Queen, 16, 87
Vintage Year (1912), 5, 7, 15-22, 29
"Vivat Les Etudiants", 7, 32-47 (chapter title), 41

W

Wana, 71, 84, 85
Walpole, Hugh, Sir, 17
Warwick Road, 25
Waziristan, 71, 84, 85
Wazirs tribe, 71, 84
Wellington, Duke of, 61
Wells, H. G., 17
Whish, General, 59
White feather, 25
Willcocks, James, Sir, Gen., 83, 87
Wimbledon, 24
Wine, 7, 15, 27, 35, 37, 40
Wood, Georgie, Wee, 17
Wood, Henry, Sir, 17
Women's Suffrage, 21
World War I. See Great War
World War II. See Second World War
Wren, Christopher, Sir, 26

Z

Zakha Khel tribe, 82, 83, 87

www.ingramcontent.com/pod-product-compliance
Lightning Source LLC
Chambersburg PA
CBHW061217070526
44584CB00029B/3872